PRIVATE PENSIONS AND EMPLOYEE MOBILITY

Recent Titles from Quorum Books

The Ethics of Organizational Transformation: Mergers, Takeovers, and Corporate Restructuring
W. Michael Hoffman, Robert Frederick, and Edward S. Petry, Jr., editors

Cable TV Advertising: In Search of the Right Formula
Rajeev Batra and Rashi Glazer, editors

The Marketer's Guide to Selling Products Abroad
Robert E. Weber

Corporate Social Responsibility: Guidelines for Top Management
Jerry W. Anderson, Jr.

Product Life Cycles and Product Management
Sak Onkvisit and John J. Shaw

Human Resource Management in the Health Care Sector: A Guide for Administrators and Professionals
Amarjit S. Sethi and Randall S. Schuler, editors

Export Strategy
Subhash C. Jain

The Protectionist Threat to Corporate America: The U.S. Trade Deficit and Management Responses
Louis E. V. Nevaer and Steven A. Deck

Environmentally Induced Cancer and the Law: Risks, Regulation, and Victim Compensation
Frank B. Cross

Legal and Economic Regulation in Marketing: A Practitioner's Guide
Ray O. Werner

Smoking and the Workplace: Issues and Answers for Human Resources Professionals
William M. Timmins and Clark Brighton Timmins

PRIVATE PENSIONS AND EMPLOYEE MOBILITY

A Comprehensive Approach to
Pension Policy

Izzet Sahin

Q

Quorum Books
New York · Westport, Connecticut · London

331.25
S 131

Library of Congress Cataloging-in-Publication Data

Sahin, Izzet.
   Private pensions and employee mobility.

   Includes index.
   1. Pensions—United States—Econometric models.
   2. Pensions—Canada—Econometric models. 3. Occupational mobility—United
States—Econometric models.
   4. Occupational mobility—Canada—Econometric models.
   I. Title.
   HD7125.S22   1989   331.25′2′0973   88-35745
   ISBN 0-89930-302-1 (lib. bdg. : alk. paper)

British Library Cataloguing in Publication Data is available.

Library of Congress Catalog Card Number: 88-35745
ISBN: 0-89930-302-1

First published in 1989 by Quorum Books

Greenwood Press, Inc.
88 Post Road West, Westport, Connecticut 06881

Printed in the United States of America

The paper used in this book complies with the Permanent Paper Standard issued by
the National Information Standards Organization (Z39.48-1984).

10 9 8 7 6 5 4 3 2 1

Contents

Figures and Tables   vii

Preface   xi

1. Background, Issues and Perspectives   1

    1.1 Pension Coverage   1
    1.2 Portability   3
    1.3 Vesting   4
    1.4 Plan Types   6
    1.5 History of Pensions in the U.S.   7
    1.6 The Canadian Experience   12
    1.7 Issues and Perspectives   17

2. Work Life Perspective   22

    2.1 Mobility   23
    2.2 Pensionable Service   31
    2.3 Pension Benefits   46

3. Plan Perspective   81

    3.1 Data and Assumptions   82
    3.2 Expected Benefits and Costs   84
    3.3 Variability and Distribution of Plan Benefits and Costs   89

3.4 Some Recent Issues—A Case Study 97
3.5 Dynamics of Pension Reform—Another Case Study 103

Index 113

About the Author 117

Figures and Tables

FIGURES

2.1 Expected work life (20 to 65) pensionable service as a function of the coverage rate (p) under different portability (π) and vesting rules(s) 45

2.2 Expected work life (20 to 65) pensionable service as a function of portability (π) under different coverage rates (p) and vesting rules(s) 47

2.3 Time parameters and periods of benefit accrual 52

2.4 Expected work life benefits in career average plans 71

2.5 Expected work life benefits in last three years' average plans 72

2.6 Expected work life benefits in money purchase plans 73

3.1 Distributions of plan benefit (plan cost) in career average plans under different cliff vesting rules 93

3.2 Distributions of plan benefit (plan cost) in final five years' average plans under different cliff vesting rules 94

3.3 Distributions of plan benefit (plan cost) in money purchase plans under different cliff vesting rules 96

3.4 Evolution of pension benefits in career average plans 105

3.5 Evolution of pension benefits in final average plans 107

3.6 Evolution of pension costs in career average plans 108

3.7 Evolution of pension costs in final average plans 109

TABLES

2.1 Actual and Fitted Termination Rates for Moderate Mobility Groups — 25

2.2 Mobility Measures — 26

2.3 Pensionable Service as a Function of Age at Entry (t) and Completed Service (X) under ERISA Vesting Standards — 34

2.4 Rank of ERISA Vesting Provisions in Terms of Expected Pensionable Service in the Plan as a Function of the Age at Entry (t) — 36

2.5 Expected Pensionable Service under ERISA Vesting Provisions — 37

2.6 Pensionable Service as a Function of Age at Entry (t) and Completed Service (X) under the 1986 Tax Reform Act Vesting Standards — 38

2.7 Expected Pensionable Service in the Plan under the 1986 Tax Reform Act Vesting Standards — 39

2.8 Mean Work Life Pensionable Service under Different Cliff Vesting Rules — 42

2.9 Accrued Benefits in Different Plans as Replacement and Reservation Rates (Moderate Mobility, Cliff-5 Vesting Rule) — 56

2.10 Expected Termination Benefits in Different Plans as Replacement and Reservation Rates (Moderate Mobility, Cliff-5 Vesting Rule) — 57

2.11 Expected Virtual Benefits in Different Plans as Replacement and Reservation Rates (Moderate Mobility, Cliff-5 Vesting Rule) — 58

2.12 Expected Termination (TB) and Virtual Benefits (VB) under Low and High Mobility Assumptions (Cliff-5 Vesting Rule) — 63

2.13 Expected Termination (TB) and Virtual Benefits (VB) under Cliff-2 and Cliff-10 Vesting Rules — 66

2.14 Expected Losses in Replacement Rates (Rep) and Reservation Wage Increases (Res) Induced by Potential Job Changes — 76

3.1 Expected Plan Benefits — 85

3.2 Expected Plan Benefits under Different Inflationary Assumptions in Noncontributory and Contributory Plans — 87

3.3 Expected Plan Costs (Employer plus Employee Costs) as a Constant Fraction of the Payroll — 90

3.4 Coefficients of Variation of Plan Benefits and Costs — 91

3.5 Pension Costs under Base Scenarios 98

3.6 Employer Costs in Contributory Plans under Improved 100
Employee Reimbursements (Reform 1) and Equal Cost
Allocation (Reform 2)

3.7 Expected Pension Costs under the Excess Interest Ad- 102
justment of Benefits in Payment (Reform 3) and Deferred Benefits (Reform 4)

Preface

Historically, discussion of private pensions in the United States and Canada has centered around the need for change and the anticipated effects of changing policies and practices. While the employers have been concerned primarily with the magnitude and predictability of pension costs as a fraction of the payroll, issues of importance to the workers have been the existence and value of pension benefits. On the other hand, governments have been concerned with the overall well being of the private pension system, as regulators through statutory vesting standards and funding requirements, and as subsidizers through tax deferrals.

From an employee's perspective, the pension component of the wage-pension mix is difficult to evaluate, even in relation to current and past employments. If one ignores mobility and assumes a single employer, one may conclude that pension plans that relate benefits to nominal earnings just before retirement provide adequate protection of benefits from inflation. For an increase in the rate of inflation is generally reflected in wage growth rates which in turn result in an upward adjustment in pension benefits by way of the earnings related benefit formula. This has been the conventional wisdom behind the favorable assessment of unit-benefit plans as a hedge against inflation. Unfortunately, this effect is greatly weakened by mobility—vested benefits will erode with inflation from employment termination to retirement.

An individual's need to properly assess pension benefits is not limited to accrued pension in the current and past employments and their value at retirement. Rational job change decisions, for example, require information also on the pension promise of the current job, if it continued until a later time, and on the wage-pension mix offered by other job prospects. Such data are even more difficult to process for the individual.

From employers' perspective, the concern is with the efficient and economical utilization of human resources. In growing industries, the pension promise is generally regarded as an important management tool for retaining labor. It is also believed, however, that the main cause of the low rates of mobility in some segments of the work force, especially in declining industries, is the expectation of a generous pension following a long job tenure. In these industries, pension expectations may have become a serious constraint on job mobility, thus creating serious labor allocation problems and high costs of retraining, severance, and early retirement.

From a public policy perspective, at issue is the effectiveness of the private pension system. Historically, pension legislation in the United States and Canada has been concerned with regulating the system on its own ground. Recent laws have affected many legal, tax, and actuarial aspects of private pensions. They established new reporting and fiduciary requirements, plan termination insurance for certain plans, and new statutory vesting requirements. They did not interfere with the basic structure of the system, however, and did not address the questions of coverage and portability. There is nothing in the current pension legislation that would oblige any employer to establish and maintain a pension plan. Although private pension benefits are expected to increase in the United States following the recent liberalization of vesting rules, it could be argued that these changes would not provide a satisfactory solution to the problem of loss in pension benefits following employment termination and would not substantially decrease the proportion of retired workers with inadequate private pension income.

Objective examination of these and other issues from the points of view of different agents requires a formalization of the processes by which private pension benefits accumulate over time. This has been the main focus of my recent research in the area. This research is based on a new approach that reverses the standard perspective of looking at the firm to determine pension obligations and to study the impact of pensions on important economic processes. Instead, the worker is taken as the unit of analysis and the evolution of costs and benefits are determined over the work life which may include several employments and membership in different pension plans. In a probabilistic framework, pension accumulation is linked to mobility, vesting, coverage, portability, plan characteristics, and other variables. The theory was first constructed around pensionable service[1] and later extended to pension benefits and costs.[2] Applications to date include studies of the private pension systems of Ontario[3] and the United States.[4]

This book provides an integrated and simplified account of my recent research. It includes substantial new material and covers a wide range of issues around the central theme of *pensions and mobility*. It differs from the conventional pension literature both in terms of methodology and emphasis. Traditionally, actuarial work in the area has been plan or firm oriented.[5] It is generally directed to the design and operation of pension plans, emphasizing pension costs and the estimation of annual contributions required to meet future liabilities.

This perspective—of firm orientation—has been prevalent also in economic research on pensions.[6] Questions related to capital accumulation, efficient allocation of labor, and income distribution at retirement have been discussed generally in the context of no mobility and a single employer. While appropriate in the analysis of social security and saving behavior, this perspective has important limitations in the case of private pensions due to certain characteristics of these arrangements. In addition to wage and benefit levels, accrual of private pension benefits is based on vesting provisions and therefore on mobility. Also, while the wage parameters entered into social security benefit calculations are indexed to inflation until retirement, in the case of private pensions there is either no indexing or only partial indexing until employment termination which may precede retirement by many years. These differences between the two systems have important consequences. It is the interaction of job mobility, inflation, vesting rules, pension coverage, and portability that results in an unequal distribution of pension benefits to individuals with comparable working lives and wage profiles. This interaction has a critical impact on almost every issue related to private pensions. To capture it, we take the worker as the unit of analysis and concentrate on the dynamics of pension accumulation.

Throughout the text, I have tried to emphasize the concepts and their application to issues. The underlying methodology is model-based and highly mathematical. The formal development of this methodology is not included; but the interested reader is directed to references that provide a more technical treatment of some of the topics. The book is addressed to all economic agents involved in the private pension system. These include employers, employees and the government. The various issues covered should be of interest to government policymakers as well as to employee and employer representatives—actuaries, accountants, employee benefit specialists and financial advisors.

NOTES

1. Izzet Sahin, "Cumulative Constrained Sojourn Times in Semi-Markov Processes with an Application to Pensionable Service," *Journal of Applied Probability*, 15 (1978), pp. 531-542.

2. Yves Balcer and Izzet Sahin, "A Stochastic Theory of Pension Dynamics," *Insurance: Mathematics and Economics*, 2 (1983), pp. 179-197.

3. Yves Balcer and Izzet Sahin, "Dynamics of Pension Reform: The Case of Ontario," *The Journal of Risk and Insurance*, 51 (1984), pp. 652-686.

4. Izzet Sahin, *Job Mobility and Private Pensions*, International Foundation of Employee Benefit Plans, Brookfield, WI, 1986.

5. See, for example, Dan M. McGill, *Fundamentals of Private Pensions*, 3d ed., Irwin, Homewood, IL, 1975.

6. For a recent treatment of important economic issues, see Richard A. Ippolito, *Pensions, Economics and Public Policy*, Dow Jones-Irwin, Homewood, IL, 1986.

PRIVATE PENSIONS AND EMPLOYEE MOBILITY

1
Background, Issues and Perspectives

There are a number of institutional and structural characteristics of private pensions that set them apart from social security. Important among these are coverage, portability, vesting provisions and plan types. As an input for later discussion, this chapter first introduces these characteristics with reference to some recent data from Canada and the United States. The historical background is next reviewed in Section 1.5 and Section 1.6 regarding the experiences of both countries, as a perspective for the evolution of modern issues. The chapter concludes with a look at some of these issues and the approach to be followed in the sequel.

1.1 PENSION COVERAGE

Pension coverage varies from one segment of the labor force to another, being more prevalent in large, unionized firms. Generally left out are workers in small nonunion enterprises and those in agriculture and self-employment. According to recent surveys,[1] 40 million workers were covered by private pensions in the United States in 1979, constituting 34 percent of the total labor force and nearly 49 percent of the total private wage and salary employees. In terms of the latter measure, the overall coverage rate increased from 24 percent in 1950 to 40 percent in 1960 and reached the current level of just below 50 percent in 1975. There has not been a significant change in private pension coverage rates since 1975. These data include active employees covered under pay-as-you-go plans, multi-employer plans, union-administered plans, deferred profit sharing plans, plans of nonprofit organizations, and railroad plans supplementing the federal railroad retirement program. They exclude plans for federal, state and local employees, employees covered under the Railroad Retirement Board Plan, and the Plan of the Federal Reserve System. Collectively, federal, state and local employment pensions cover another 14 percent of the total labor force.[2] They also exclude tax-sheltered annuity plans and plans for the self-employed.

The likelihood of pension coverage is higher among males, older workers, well-educated workers and workers with high earnings. Cross tabulations of pension coverage with respect to these variables[3] show that sex and age have generally independent effects on coverage. Pension coverage rates increase with age until age 60, when close to 70 percent of working males but only 42 percent of females are covered.[4] There are also substantial positive correlations between pension coverage and education, and pension coverage and earnings level. In 1979, nearly 62 percent of males with 17 or more years of schooling reported pension coverage, compared with 42 percent of males with under 9 years of schooling;[5] this relation also holds for females and for all age groups. Also, while 66 percent of males of age 51 to 65 were covered by pensions in 1979, only a third of these earned below $5,000 a year. Similarly, coverage rates for males earning $10,000 to $15,000 and for those earning over $25,000 were 61 percent and 80 percent, respectively.[6] These data also show that the male-female differentials in coverage rates are largely explainable by earnings differentials.

In terms of industrial patterns, coverage rates are highest in transportation and utilities (65 percent) followed by manufacturing (64 percent). The next two largest industries, services and retail trade, had 1979 coverage rates of 29 percent and 24 percent, respectively.[7] Pension coverage rate was the lowest in agriculture at about 12 percent.

Generally similar rates and patterns also prevail in Canada. About 48 percent of the Canadian work force were members of employment pension plans in 1980.[8] Most of these plans, involving about 90 percent of the labor force, fell under provincial jurisdiction, while the federal government was responsible for the regulation of the remaining 10 percent. Excluding public sector workers, where the coverage rate is 95 percent, about 47 percent of men and 22 percent of women working in the private sector are covered by an employment pension.[9] Younger workers and low income earners had the least coverage. Comparisons of these numbers with the results of earlier surveys show that coverage rates may have stabilized also in Canada. The fraction of covered workers increased from 42 percent in 1970 to 48 percent in 1978; it dropped marginally in 1980.[10]

Recent forecasts commissioned by the U.S. Department of Labor do not indicate any significant increase in coverage rates in the future under current policies.[11] This near stagnation of the coverage rate at about the 50 percent level is attributed to the fact that the coverage rate is already high in some of the large industries, such as manufacturing and transportation. Most economic forecasts predict that these industries will have a declining share of the labor force in the future. On the other hand, low pension coverage industries, such as services and trade, are predicted to grow. The general decline in unionization and the power of labor unions may have also contributed to the leveling off of the private pension coverage rates. Emergence of alternative vehicles and sources of retirement income, such as the Individual Retirement Accounts (IRAs) in the U.S. and the Registered Retirement Savings Plans (RRSPs) in Canada could also be a contributing factor.

Pension coverage we discussed above may be characterized as point-in-time coverage. Although it has been the center of much public debate for a long time, this measure has important shortcomings. It does not take into account whether the pension being accrued will be forfeited due to stringent vesting rules or, even though the pension is vested, whether its value will be eroded away by inflation. Also, point-in-time coverage data make no distinction between generous pension plans and those with poor benefits, and between "portable" pensions and those that are not transferable. We now look at these additional characteristics.

1.2 PORTABILITY

Portability refers to the transferability of pension rights and the underlying assets from one employment to the next, irrespective of the vesting status. Large plans, union plans, and multi-employer plans are more likely to feature portability. Intrasystem portability without loss of vesting rights is a characteristic of almost half of the multi-employer plans. Intersystem portability and portability between single employer and multi-employer plans are less common. Only 21 percent of the single employer plans reported portability in 1977.[12] It is very likely, however, that this level is a gross overestimate, as portability is often confused with vesting, reciprocity, or even with an employee's potential use of an IRA. In terms of industrial patterns, portability is the most common feature of plans in construction, followed by retail trade, by transportation, communication and utilities, and by mining.[13] On the other hand, portability is less typical of plans in agriculture, forestry and fishing, in manufacturing, and in services.[14] Unfortunately, recent data on exact levels of portability by industry are not reliable due to reporting biases mentioned above.

Of the two features of private pension plans that are commonly—and incorrectly—associated with portability, vesting and reciprocity, the latter refers to a transfer of pension rights *without* a corresponding transfer of the underlying assets. Clearly, in order to avoid a financial disadvantage to any of the participants, there should be a near balance between the plans involved in a reciprocity agreement in terms of intrasystem mobility. It is also clear, on general grounds, that all the pension plans that participate in such an arrangement should have similar or identical characteristics. Because of the technical complications that these requirements create, reciprocity has not extended in practice beyond particular unions or closely comparable employer groups. For example, there is usually reciprocity between different public sector retirement plans in a state, but almost none between different state and federal employment.

On the other hand, in as much as the underlying assets are also transferred, portability may appear to be more easily applicable than reciprocity. It might also be seen as a desirable feature in reducing the administrative expenses involved in maintaining large numbers of records for vested termination benefits that are not transferred out of a plan. The practice of successive asset transfers would ultimately result in a very simple situation of a single pension to be sponsored by the last employer. However, although less of a theoretical proposition than reciprocity agreements, widespread practice of portability is constrained by difficulties of asset valuation and incompatible plan types.

In the sequel, portability (or lack of it) will emerge as a central theme in many issues. We shall see, however, that its impact on pension benefits and costs cannot be assessed in isolation. Rather, it should be examined in relation to other characteristics of employment pensions.

1.3 VESTING

In almost all private pension plans in North America, upon termination of an employment covered by a pension plan, an employee is entitled to pension benefits at retirement, subject to a minimum length of *service requirement*. In addition, some pension plans also feature an *age requirement* in terms of a prescribed minimum age on separation. If these provisions are met, then the pension is said to be *vested* in the employee in that the employee collects benefits from it upon retirement even if he or she never again works for that organization. Otherwise, the employee is generally entitled only to a return of his or her own contributions. These provisions are called *vesting rules*, and a length of service that meets them is referred to as *pensionable service*.

Vesting rules are subject to government regulation. In the United States, the Employee Retirement Income Security Act (ERISA) of 1974 allows the sponsors of a pension plan to select one of three vesting rules in satisfaction of the minimum vesting requirements. The first is full vesting (sometimes referred to as "cliff" vesting) after ten years of service. The second involves graded vesting (or "graduated" vesting), providing 25 percent vesting after five years of service which increases by five percentage points per year for the next five years and ten percentage points per year for the next five years. This schedule results in vesting after 15 years of service. The third minimum vesting provision allowed under ERISA is known as the "Rule of 45." This method provides for 50 percent vesting after the earlier of ten years of service or when the combination of service (minimum of five years) and the employee's age total 45. Thereafter, the employee's vested interest increases ten percentage points per year for the next five years.

In Canada, regulation of the private pension system falls under provincial jurisdiction. Under the Ontario Pension Benefits Act of 1965, which was subsequently adopted by most of the other Canadian provinces and the federal government, the age and service requirements for vesting may not be more stringent than 45 years and 10 years, respectively.

Although permitted by law to the above extent, the age requirement for vesting has been gradually losing its prominence. United States, Canada, and several Canadian provinces have recently adopted more liberal statutory vesting rules than those mentioned above that do not involve any age requirement. In the United States, under the Tax Reform Act of 1986, all tax-qualified employment pension plans (other than multi-employer plans) must meet one of the two minimum vesting standards: full vesting after 5 years of service, or a graded vesting providing 20 percent after 3 years plus 20 percent for each additional year until full vesting after 7 years of service.

At the present time, a majority of private pension plans in North America feature the vesting rule of 10 years of service. In the United States the participant-weighted mean (PAM) years until full vesting was 9.35 in 1977; the corresponding plan-weighted mean (PLM) was 7.46 years.[15] Vesting rules tend to be more liberal in defined contribution plans (PAM = 7.14, PLM = 6.76) than in defined benefit plans[16] (PAM = 10.01, PLM = 9.06) and in nonunion plans (PAM = 8.97, PLM = 7.25) than in union plans[17] (PAM = 9.73, PLM = 9.85). The main cause of the latter is that nonunion workers and plans are more likely to have immediate vesting than union workers and plans. Also, union workers are more likely to be covered by large plans featuring 10-year cliff vesting, while small plans having various graded vesting rules are more typical of nonunion workers. In terms of industrial patterns, while there are substantial differences from one industry to another regarding proportions of plans with different vesting rules, there is little variation on the fractions of participants covered by each vesting rule, because small plans are accountable for most of the differences across industries. Thus the plan-weighted mean years of service until full vesting varied in 1977 from 6.77 for the agriculture to 10.02 for the manufacturing, while the range for the participant-weighted mean was from 8.95 for the transportation to 10.94 for the mining industries.[18]

Vesting requirements may be viewed as instruments for the firm in reducing both labor mobility and the cost of administering the pension plan. The age requirement defers membership in the plan for new employees, decreasing the short run administrative costs. The service requirement denies the worker nonforfeitable benefits for an additional period, reducing the employee turnover in the longer run. However, by prolonging an employee's obligation to the firm and by increasing the risk of benefit forfeitures, delayed vesting may result in inefficiencies in labor allocation and may affect pension accumulation adversely. These effects are compounded by limited pension coverage, lack of portability, high labor mobility and inflation. Although much has been said and written about their individual impact on pension benefits and related issues, the interactive effects of these factors are not well understood.

1.4 PLAN TYPES

Private pension benefits and costs also depend on the plan type. In general, there are two categories: *defined benefit* plans and *defined contribution* plans. In turn a defined benefit plan may be either a *unit benefit* plan or a *flat benefit* plan. In unit benefit plans, pension benefits are determined by taking a specified percentage (called the benefit level) of the remuneration of an employee for each year (i.e., *career average* plans) or for a selected number of years of service (i.e., *final average* plans). In flat benefit plans, pension benefits are expressed as a fixed amount for each year of pensionable service. In defined contribution plans, pension benefits are determined on retirement by the accumulated amount of past contributions, made according to a specified contribution level, and by the returns on investment.

A large majority of private pension participants are covered by defined benefit plans which are generally favored by large firms and in unionized industries. Defined contribution plans are more prevalent among small employers, partnerships and the nonprofit sector. Almost equal fractions of defined benefit plan participants are enrolled in unit benefit and flat benefit plans. In terms of the earnings base used in benefit calculations, the most popular unit benefit plan type is the final (or best) five years' average plan, followed by career average, ten-year final average, and three-year final average plans.[19] In most flat benefit plans, the accrued benefit is based on the length of service. But flat benefit plans that are based on neither earnings nor service also account for a significant proportion of the defined benefit plan membership.

Contrary to the general belief that defined benefit plans provide some protection from inflation—at least until termination of employment—flat benefit plans with their benefit formulas unrelated to earnings are technically exposed to inflation. Their popularity, therefore, especially among union-negotiated plans, may be surprising; however, the benefit amounts in most flat benefit plans are periodically raised to reflect the growth in wages. In this respect most flat benefit plans function in reality as unit benefit plans. In addition to exposure to inflation, defined benefit plans have a number of drawbacks, as well as advantages, both from the points of view of employers and employees.

Also of some relevance to a number of issues is the contributory-noncontributory differentiation of pension plans. A plan is *noncontributory* if only the employer contributes to the fund (on behalf of employees), but *contributory* if both the employer and the employees contribute. If pensions are viewed as deferred wages, the distinction may be viewed as not essential. It has been of historical importance, however, in relation to the question of who has the right to manage and control the pension fund. Earlier plans were all noncontributory plans established and controlled by employers. Although there has been a steady trend towards contributory plans, noncontributory plans still dominate the scene.

1.5 HISTORY OF PENSIONS IN THE U.S.

American Express Company was the first United States corporation to provide a formal pension plan for its employees in 1875; however, pension coverage was something of a rarity until the turn of the century. The period of greatest earlier growth was between 1900 and 1920. By 1910, there were about sixty plans and the railroads, public utilities, banks, and the larger industrial corporations provided most of these.[20] During the next decade, new plans were established at a somewhat faster rate. This is attributed to the scientific management movement, recognition of labor turnover, and tax advantages first made available in 1916.[21] After 1920, the growth rate declined, however, and did not show a significant increase until the postwar years.

The early plans failed to deal with the problem of old age dependency at an adequate level. They usually required 15 to 30 years of service and only a few plans legally obligated the company to any payment at all.[22] Most of them were noncontributory plans and therefore did not offer even the advantages of accumulated forced savings. This policy of providing noncontributory plans was believed to have a number of advantages for the employers. Also, except for a very small number of contributory plans, early pension arrangements did not provide for the vesting of employee benefits following terminations before retirement. Benefits were typically based on wage and length of service. The final average design, with an earnings base of one to ten years, were quite common among the earlier plans. However, the high-inflation period of 1916–1920 raised some concern with the high costs of final average plans and these fell out of favor during the mid-1920s.[23] None of the early plans provided any adjustment to pension benefits for inflation. Most of them were financed on a pay-as-you-go basis; 60 percent of noncontributory plans in 1929, for example, were financed by the employer's current income, 25 percent had a balance sheet reserve for pension costs, and only 15 percent had established a trust fund or were using insured arrangements.[24] According to one estimate, the typical pension plan of the 1920s paid the retired worker about half of what the lowest paid government worker received.[25]

1.5.1 Railroad Plans and Social Security

Federal government regulation of the pension industry goes back to the early 1920s. Until the mid-1930s, however, this was limited to the tax treatment of pension trusts and employee contributions. The years 1934 and 1935 mark the beginning of substantial federal government involvement in pensions and old age security. Both the Railroad Retirement Act of 1935 and the Social Security Act of 1935 have been profoundly influential in determining the course of the pension industry.

The railroad industry was a pioneer in providing pension plans for retired and disabled workers. By 1922, more than 80 percent of the railroad personnel were covered by these plans which typically allowed retirement at the age of 70 with at least 20 years of continuous service.[26] Almost none of these plans was adequately funded, however, and they could not be sustained during the depression years in the face of sharply declining railroad revenues. During the late 1920s and early 1930s railroad companies laid off about 800,000 employees.[27] This did not reduce the pension burden much, however, due to the retention of those with long job tenures; in 1934 about 250,000 (25 percent) of the active railroad personnel were over 60 years old or had served 30 years or more.[28] It seemed virtually impossible for the industry to keep the pension promise for these people and there was strong public pressure for the federal government to step in. In June 1934, the Wagner-Hatfield Railroad Retirement Bill was passed by both houses and signed by President Roosevelt. The main objectives of the legislation were to reduce unemployment by retiring 50,000 workers immediately and to provide a testing ground for a general program of social security, then under serious consideration. It was not the intent of the legislation to provide security for the retired workers.[29] In October 1934 the act was declared unconstitutional by the District of Columbia Supreme Court, on the grounds that it affected employees not engaged directly in interstate commerce, and in May 1935 it was voided by the Supreme Court.

Aside from constitutionality, the petitioning of the Wagner-Hatfield Act by the carriers, the rulings that followed, and the debate surrounding these signify the beginning of the end for two traditional objectives of pension legislation: retirement of the aged inefficient workers, and unemployment relief. In August 1935, Roosevelt signed into law a restructured Railroad Retirement Act. In this process, dropped were the arguments of efficiency and unemployment relief. Rather, taxing power and the general welfare clause of the constitution were emphasized and "the ideology of social security was given formal sanction."[30]

The Social Security Act was also passed in August 1935 and signed by Roosevelt. He described the act as "a law that will take care of human needs and at the same time provide for the United States an economic structure of vastly greater soundness." The act was substantially redesigned by a series of amendments in 1939 which, among other changes, added survivors' benefits. However, the benefit amounts stayed very low during the war years and then until the 1950s. Benefit levels were increased ten different times by ad hoc legislation from 1950 to 1972.[31] Other changes made during this period included widening of the Social Security coverage to include self-employed workers, Americans employed abroad by American employers, the armed forces, and, on an elective basis, state and local government employees, whether or not they are covered by a retirement system. By 1958, total disability benefits were added for workers of all ages. Medicare for people of age 65 and older was included in 1965, thus completing the present day Social Security program involving old age, survivors, disability and health care benefits.

1.5.2 Postwar Years

Private, state and local pensions grew rapidly during the postwar years as a response to changes in the family support of the elderly, an expansion of the retirement period, and an increasing uncertainty about the extent to which old age benefits under Social Security can provide for the retirement years. This growth was also encouraged by some wartime tax legislation. Under the excess profits tax of 1940, pension plans became an ideal mechanism to defer corporate income from high to low tax years. The Revenue Act of 1942 and the related Treasury Department regulations enabled pension plans to provide greater payments to higher income groups.[32] Thus the increase in private pension coverage after the early 1940s was in part due to income tax advantages brought about by deferred compensation which was also exempt from wartime wage controls.[33]

Private plans covered 4.1 million workers in 1940, 6.4 million in 1945 and 9.8 million in 1950; employers were allocating 17 percent of the payroll to pension payments by 1946.[34]

Main lines of the modern legislation regarding the federal regulation of private pensions also emerged during the war years. The objectives were to develop legislation to serve broader employee welfare and to avoid the use of employee trusts primarily as tax deferral devices. In 1942, the Department of the Treasury proposed that in order to qualify for tax-exempt status, pension trusts should be required to meet three basic standards regarding vesting, coverage and maximum benefits.[35] The original proposal suggested immediate vesting; this was later modified to graded vesting, starting at age 40 and 15 years' membership in the plan, and then dropped altogether in view of opposition both by labor and management.[36] Sections of the Internal Revenue Code dealing with pension plans were completely revised, however, and rewritten to ensure that, in order to qualify for the statutory tax treatment, pension and profit sharing trusts met certain requirements. Specifically, a plan that was required to be for the purpose of providing retirement benefit for its members had to be nondiscriminatory as between its members, and its assets could not be diverted elsewhere before meeting the liabilities to the employees and their beneficiaries.[37] Thus the Code addressed the area of pension plan provisions for the first time.

Another important development of the 1940s was the emergence of pensions as proper subjects for collective bargaining under the Taft-Hartly Act of 1947. Shortly after the passage of the act, a dispute arose between the steelworkers' union and the Inland Steel Company as to whether the act imposed an obligation on the part of the employers to include pensions in collective bargaining. Earlier, in late 1945, the Amalgamated Clothing Workers of America had reached an agreement with clothing manufacturers on a pension plan covering 150,000 workers.[38] Also, the United Mine Workers had struck in 1946 over the retirement fund issue.[39] Eventually, the National Labor Relations Board ruled in April 1948 that the companies were required to bargain on pension plans, on the grounds that the definition of "wages" in the Taft-Hartley Act included pension benefits and a pension plan was a "condition of employment."[40] This ruling was later affirmed by the federal courts, following the appeal of the Inland Steel Company.

These developments mark the beginning of a period of active involvement of unions in matters related to pension plans and pension benefits. AFL-CIO affiliates joined the rush of collective bargaining which resulted in more than 5 million workers covered by union negotiated plans by 1955.[41] Although these organizations still favored increases in Social Security benefits rather than in private pension benefits, they were no longer as skeptical of employment pensions as they were during the earlier decades; they did not view them as "paternalistic devices" introduced to hold down wages.

1.5.3 Growth Years and ERISA

During the next three decades (1950-1980), private pension coverage was more than doubled from 16 percent to 35 percent of the total labor force.[42] Coverage under the Social Security system also increased drastically during this period from 59 percent to about 85 percent of the labor force.[43] However, this period of steady growth and gradual liberalization (of vesting rules and benefit formulas) was not without difficulties. In late 1950s there was a need to strengthen the Taft-Hartley protection of pension plan members from financial mismanagement. For this purpose, the Welfare and Pension Plans Disclosure Act of 1958 was enacted. This act required that the plans qualifying under the Internal Revenue Code file a disclosure report every year with the Secretary of Labor.[44] In the 1960s and 1970s some private plans and many state and municipal retirement programs were experiencing serious funding problems. Potential losses in pension expectations became increasingly worrisome to many individuals, exemplified by heavy losses associated with the closing of the Studebaker plant in South Bend, Indiana, in 1964.

During the course of a decade of public debate following these developments, the questions of vesting, portability and proper funding of pension plans attracted a great deal of attention. The pension plans that were created during the expansion years usually required 15 or more years of service for vesting; many also had an age requirement of 40 or 50 years. In the face of high labor mobility that was associated with an increasingly service-oriented economy, this resulted in a high rate of benefit forfeitures especially in the case of younger workers. Even after vesting, most younger workers could look forward to very little in the way of pension benefit under defined benefit plans due to lack of indexation; the nominal benefit promised by the plan as a fraction of the wage at termination had very little value at retirement after many years. Many terminating employees under these plans selected the option of a return of their own contributions, if the plan was contributory. These returns carried little or no interest.

In 1965, a presidential Committee on Corporate Pension Funds and Other Private Retirement and Welfare Programs issued a report that contained various legislative recommendations regarding vesting standards, funding requirements and fiduciary protection. The Congressional hearings that followed led to a number of pension reform proposals. These in turn were followed by further studies and additional hearings and debate; and, on September 2, 1974, the Employee Retirement Income Security Act (ERISA) was signed into law. This act has made a fundamental change in the framework within which private pension plans operate from a tax-based orientation to an employee security orientation. It established new requirements in almost every phase of private pensions, including eligibility and vesting standards, funding rules, and disclosure and fiduciary responsibilities. It also established the Pension Benefit Guaranty Corporation within the Labor Department to protect plan members in the case of termination of an underfunded plan. The act covered all private plans, except for church-related plans, but not the public employee plans.

In terms of participation requirements, ERISA stipulates that the participation of a worker in a pension plan cannot be delayed beyond the later of age 25 or one year of service. Also, the maximum age restriction for membership in a plan is limited by ERISA to new employees who are within five years of the plan's normal retirement age. In terms of vesting rules, as already mentioned before, ERISA restricted the choice to one of three rules: full vesting after ten years of service, graded vesting from 5 to 15 years of service and the "Rule of 45." Under the act, plan members have a legal claim to pension benefits when their employment is pensionable according to the vesting rule chosen. In the event of a plan termination, vested benefits constitute a senior claim on the pension fund's assets. If these assets are insufficient to meet vested liabilities, firm's assets may be used to supplement them. The residual liability, if any, is insured by the Pension Benefit Guaranty Corporation. On the other hand, nonvested workers who leave the firm before retirement have no legal claim to future pension benefits. In the event of plan termination, such benefits constitute a claim only on the pension fund, secondary to vested benefits.

The minimum vesting provisions imposed on private pension plans are further liberalized by the Tax Reform Act of 1986. According to this act, all tax-qualified private pension funds, other than multi-employer plans, must meet one of the following minimum vesting standards: full vesting after 5 years of service, or 20 percent vesting after 3 years of service plus 20 percent for each additional year until 100 percent after 7 years of service. Multi-employer plans must provide full vesting after 10 years of service. These provisions will be effective for plan years beginning in 1989 (or as late as 1991 for collectively bargained plans) and applicable to both past and future benefits earned under the plan. The act also defined new nondiscrimination standards and new rules regarding integration with social security, and introduced other changes in the Internal Revenue Code involving pensions.

1.6 THE CANADIAN EXPERIENCE

The need for better and more specific measures to protect the interests of employees in pension plans had also become apparent in Canada by late

1950s. At that time, a limited number of pension plans covered a small fraction of the labor force. Many employees who worked for employers with plans could not join due to restrictions on entry, age requirements and lenghty service requirements. Even for enrolled workers, the pension promise did not come to fruition because of mobility and stringent vesting requirements. Pension plans set up economic forces that reduced employment opportunities for older workers; some plans did not accept members over the age of 45 or 50.[45] Government supervision and inspection were minimal and uneven. In 1950, new federal income tax rules on pension plans provided for the vesting of the employer's contributions after 20 years' membership in a plan and the attainment of age 50.[46] In 1959, new rules were announced, however, and the vesting rules were discontinued on constitutional grounds.[47] With this and other areas of regulation vacated by the federal government, Ontario was the leading province to step in to formulate a provincial policy on pensions and to introduce legislation. The Committee on Portable Pensions was appointed for this purpose in 1960. The major issue facing this committee was how a worker might move from one job to another without losing pension rights.

The Committee on Portable Pensions issued its final report and a draft bill in July 1961. Convinced that the expansion of pension plans would not proceed quickly and far enough to meet the social needs unless government inducement or compulsion were involved, the committee recommended that all employers with 15 or more employees be obligated to introduce pension plans and that vesting be required on a graded basis starting at age 30 with 20 percent vesting, increasing by 20 percentage points a year.[48] The committee also found that many plans would not have sufficient assets if the employer ceased operation and recommended that pension plans, together with their annual statements of assets, liabilities, and incomes, be filed in a government office and that an actuarial certificate be required every few years.

Based on the recommendations of the Committee on Portable Pensions, Ontario introduced legislation in 1963 "to provide for the extension, improvement, and solvency of pension plans and for the portability of pension benefits."[49] The legislation required employers with more than 15 employees to establish a "standard plan" that would provide for eligibility between the ages of 30 and 70 and the payment of a pension benefit at age 70. The plan could use a career average formula with a benefit level of 0.5 percent of wage up to $400 per month for each year of eligible service; a money purchase formula of 1.5 percent, 2 percent and 3 percent at ages 30, 45 and 55, respectively, of the first $400 of remuneration per month with interest of not less than 4 percent; or a flat benefit formula of $2 a month for each year of eligible service. The act also provided for the establishment of the Pension Commission of Ontario, the registration of plans, funding a pension plan to assure solvency, immediate vesting at age

30 in the standard plan, and authority to establish a central pension agency to hold pension benefits transferred from employment plans when employees with vested rights changed jobs. Supplementary plans could also have been registered to provide additional benefits. These plans had to provide for a deferred annuity at termination of employment for anyone who had reached the age of 45 and who had been an employee for 10 years.

The provisions of this legislation regarding the compulsory establishment of a standard plan were repealed in 1964 as a result of federal-provincial negotiations leading to the enactment of the Canada Pension Plan in 1965.[50] The balance of the legislation came into effect as the Pension Benefits Act of 1965, the provincial statute under which employment pension plans in Ontario have been regulated until recently. The act kept the other features of the original legislation such as the establishment of the Pension Commission of Ontario, the "45 and 10" vesting rule, and the requirement to report and fund pension promises as specified by regulations.

Although the legislation in place was functioning well in terms of its original purpose, the private sector was again encountering heated criticism in the 1970s for its inability to provide adequate pensions. Some of the shortcomings identified prior to its inception by the Committee on Portable Pensions were still apparent. Pension coverage in the private sector had stabilzed around 40 percent and portability was lacking. In addition, it was becoming increasingly difficult for private plans to maintain the real value of pensions during an inflationary environment. This fact, together with the presence of full indexation in Canada Pension Plan as well as in federal and provincial public employee pension plans, was causing public dissatisfaction with private sector plans. Although it was regarded as a substantial improvement in 1965, the statutory vesting rule of "45 and 10" was now considered too stringent. Other issues were being introduced into the debate, such as whether stringent vesting rules may inhibit job mobility and whether defined benefit plans are discriminatory to younger and more mobile workers.

The Royal Commission on the Status of Pensions in Ontario was established in April 1977. The commission was directed to study the impact on the economy of different systems of financing pension plans, to examine the terms and conditions of existing plans, and to evaluate their effectiveness in terms of current social and economic circumstances.[51] In response to these charges, the commission examined in detail every source of retirement income in Ontario, conducted extensive hearings, and sponsored a number of studies and surveys. The Commission's Report, submitted to the Ontario government in 1980, constitutes a comprehensive assessment of the pension system in Ontario in terms of its components, purpose and functioning, and what might be done to improve its adequacy and effectiveness. Within this framework, the commission formulated a long list of recommendations dealing with every aspect of the pension system involving government retirement income programs and private and public sector employment pension plans.

Important among these was the recommendation that the government institute by legislation a mandatory retirement savings plan for all workers in Ontario aged 18 to 64. Called the Provincial Universal Retirement System (PURS), this plan was to be based on a money purchase design with immediate vesting and complete portability. Contribution rates for the PURS were to be determined by the government, based on the percentage of the average industrial wage it desired to be replaced when the plan matured. Targeted to a 20 percent replacement rate, and based on commission's most probable economic assumptions, the commission recommended employee contribution rates of 1, 1.5 and 2 percent for age groups 18 to 30, 30 to 45, and 45 to 65, respectively, and an employer contribution of 2 percent throughout.

There are certain parallels between the "standard plan" concept of the 1961 Committee on Portable Pensions and PURS. As noted earlier, the former was preempted by the Canada Pension Plan (CPP) introduced in 1965. It might have been more natural, therefore, to advocate the expansion of CPP rather than to advance a new mandatory plan. The Royal Commission rejected this option, however, primarily on the grounds of adverse economic consequences for the future that might arise from expanding a pay-as-you-go system.[52]

While the Ontario Commission strongly favored PURS, it also recognized that the institution of a compulsory plan for all workers might not be politically feasible. Therefore, the commission formulated different recommendations for specific provisions of existing employment pension plans depending on whether or not PURS is adopted. In particular, the commission recommended that if PURS is not adopted, then "the Pension Benefits Act should be amended to provide that the minimum vesting in all employment pension plans be upon completion of five years' continuous service with an employer or five years' membership in the pension plan, and that there be no age requirement."[53] The commission also concluded that improved vesting, with or without a mandatory plan, would not solve the following problems that arise at termination of employment: (1) in contributory defined benefit plans, it is not clear how much, if any, of the employer contributions is involved in providing the vested pension; (2) in all plans, after termination of an employee's participation status, the value of the vested pension does not increase; and (3) refunds for employees who terminate before vesting may include no interest or interest at low rates. The commission formulated several recommendations to alleviate these problems.[54]

In relation to the impact of inflation on retirement income, the commission argued that as inflation affects everyone, especially those on fixed income, it would not be appropriate to use government compulsion to ameliorate the position of only those who are members of employment pension plans. The commission considered the tax system the logical place to turn for an equitable answer and recommended the introduction of a refundable Inflation Tax Credit (ITC) for all retired residents of Ontario, starting at age 68.[55] The purpose of ITC would have been to protect from inflation that part of the eligible retirement income above the amount already fully indexed through Old Age Security (OAS), Guaranteed Income Supplement (GIS) and CPP, up to a maximum amount. Income eligible for ITC was to include employment pensions, matured Registered Retirement Savings Plans, Deferred Profit Sharing Plans, disability pensions and Workmen's Compensation.

Aside from ITC, the commission concluded that the effects of the inflation should be borne by the individual except as modified by means arrived at by employers and employees through the collective bargaining process, and by ad hoc adjustments by employers in pension plans. Many pension plan sponsors had already advocated the practice of making postretirement adjustments out of gains to pension funds arising from earnings in excess of those assumed in forecasting costs. Such gains could be made available to adjust pension benefits rather than to reduce employer costs. The commission supported a limited approach to this use of the "excess interest" concept to support pensions already in payment.

Following the report and recommendations of the Royal Commission, the public policy consensus that emerged in Ontario was in the direction of strengthening employment pension plans. The commission's recommendations regarding earlier vesting, payment of realistic interest rates on returned employee contributions, and payment by the employer of at least one-half of the deferred annuity in contributory defined benefit plans were all favored. On the other hand, recommendations for a mandatory employer pension plan and an inflation tax credit were not supported. Instead, adjustment through "excess interest" of deferred benefits as well as benefits in payment found growing acceptance as a complex but feasible and conceptually sound means of providing a degree of inflation protection. By mid-1981, a number of policy initiatives were being considered central by the Ontario government to any package of pension reforms designed to improve the effectiveness of employment pension plans.

These points were further studied and debated during 1981-1982. The reform legislation, revising the 1965 Pension Benefits Act was eventually passed in 1986. This legislation generally reflects some of the recommendations made by the Royal Commission in their 1980 report to the Ontario government. In terms of the reform issues noted above, the 1986 act mandates eligibility, entitlement and full vesting after two continuous years of service or membership in the plan. This represents a more liberal provision than the 5-year rule that was extensively examined and discussed during 1979–1981; it arose as a result of federal-provincial coordination regarding pension policy and pension legislation. Also mandated by the new act is the requirement that at least 50 percent of the cost of benefits in defined benefit plans be met by employer contributions. The new legislation covered, in addition, the payment of a fair rate of interest on returned employee contributions, but it did not address the issue of indexation. On the other hand, portability provision of the 1965 act was substantially liberalized by mandating transferability to either another pension plan or a Registered Retirement Savings Plan; a deferred life annuity could also be purchased with the proceeds.

All of these provisions are also included in the Pension Benefits Standards Act enacted by the federal government in January 1987. The federal pension legislation applies to pension plans administered for the benefit of employees in certain federal works, undertakings, and businesses. There is almost full conformity between the federal pension legislation, Ontario legislation, and the legislation pending in Nova Scotia. Manitoba, Alberta, Quebec, Saskatchewan and Newfoundland have also introduced reform legislation during recent years that features varying degrees of commonality with the federal-Ontario package. Exceptions in terms of conformity are New Brunswick and Prince Edward Island. No provincial pension legislation exists in British Columbia.

1.7 ISSUES AND PERSPECTIVES

The primary aim of a pension plan is to provide retirement income to its members. It is generally accepted that at low to moderate income levels, a preretirement income equivalency would be attained by a postretirement income of about 75 percent of the preretirement total. In the United States, the Social Security primary benefit can account for about 40 percent of the final earnings in these income groups, leaving 35 percent substantially to private pension benefits. Can the private pension system deliver such a replacement ratio? If not, what are the required changes under which reasonable expectations could be met? What are the incremental benefits and costs implied by a given liberalization in a pension plan or a pension system? How would these benefits and costs vary with mobility, periods of employment and economic conditions? More generally, what are the tradeoffs between the fundamental determinants of pension benefits and costs reflecting regulation (vesting rules, funding requirements), market response (plan types, benefit levels, coverage, portability) and individual response (employee mobility)? These questions are of vital importance to the functioning and effectiveness of employment pensions in delivering the promised benefits; however, pensions have become much more than merely arrangements for the provisioning of retirement income. They have come to play an increasingly important role in shaping social conditions and altering economic behavior.

Western economies are currently experiencing another major shift in industrial composition. The level of job mobility that is accompanying this transition is substantially lower than that which accompanied earlier transitions. For many reasons, some of which are not well understood, there is considerable resistance to job changes among workers, especially among older ones. Apparently, many such workers are willing to risk possible permanent unemployment in a declining industry, rather than risk starting over in a more stable or growing industry. Consequently, there is increasing pressure to develop programs for workers who did not change jobs before they became unemployed.

The full range of monetary incentives that encourages workers to remain too long in declining industries has not been fully explored. Paramount among these incentives that may work against appropriate job mobility patterns are workers' pensions. In most occupations, real earnings peak at a fairly early age and the subsequent primary increase in earnings occurs through the growth of pension benefits. At age 45, with 15 years on the job, a pension beginning at age 60 is likely to constitute a significant proportion of a worker's remaining lifetime compensation.

The greatest industrial shifts are occurring in the mining and manufacturing sectors. In these sectors, private pensions are more common than in almost any other industry. Virtually all steel workers, auto workers and more than half of the miners in the United States are covered by a private pension plan. These plans are seemingly generous, but they lack flexibility and portability. As a consequence, the pension vehicle that was such an important management tool for retaining labor when these industries were growing may now be becoming a major obstacle to labor's smooth exit from these industries.

Thus at issue is the measurement of the extent to which workers in various industries face disincentives to changing jobs because of an interest in pension benefits. What are the wage-pension mix differentials in a potential job change? How do these differences depend on tenure, plan types and periods of employment? What is the impact of portability (or lack of it) in determining the reservation wage of a worker in his or her job change decisions? If the workers respond to the structural characteristics of a pension system so as to attain a target replacement rate at retirement, what are the implications of a more flexible system in terms of labor mobility?

Private pensions raise important questions for employers also. Since the enactment of ERISA, the private pension system has grown rapidly. Between 1975 and 1987 the total number of pension plans has more than doubled and assets have grown from $290 billion to $1.5 trillion.[56] As a result of this rapid growth, the stake of employers as well as employees in the system has increased. While employees have been concerned with the value of their pension benefits, employers have been encountering serious difficulties in funding their rapidly growing pension obligations. Thus, what is the incremental cost of a more flexible and portable pension plan? How do pension costs vary with inflation and wage growth? What are the impacts of delayed vesting and portability? What types of plans place the least constraint on mobility? What is the happy medium between reducing employee mobility with generous but structured pension plan provisions that reward long-service employees and allowing for the natural exit of these employees, especially during periods of decline?

In what follows, we investigate these and other issues on the basis of a new and nontraditional methodology. This approach reverses—but does not preclude—the standard perspective of looking at the firm to determine pension benefits and obligations. Instead, we take the worker as the unit of analysis and determine how benefits evolve over the work life. Called the *work life perspective*, this approach and its applications are the subject matter of Chapter 2. In Chapter 3, we argue that, subject to the compatibility of the age distributions of entering and leaving employees, our methodology is also applicable at the firm level. This involves an implicit integration along age-tenure cohorts and leads to the *plan perspective* of this chapter.

Another important departure from the conventional methodology concerns the nature of the modeling framework. Here we take a probabilistic approach to the characterization of the process of pension accumulation. This permits us to generate a wealth of information without unreasonable data requirements. Throughout the book we make references to not only the expected values but also to the variances of a large number of benefit and cost measures. We are also able to construct the probability distribution of pension benefits and costs under different plan types. These distributions provide valuable information about the benefit and cost outliers.

NOTES

1. L. J. Kotlikoff and D. E. Smith, *Pensions in the American Economy*, The University of Chicago Press, Chicago, IL, 1983, pp. 163-171, 209-244.
2. Ibid., pp. 30-33.
3. Ibid., pp. 36-49.
4. Ibid., p. 37.
5. Ibid., p. 38.
6. Ibid., p. 39.
7. Ibid., pp. 45-46.

8. *Better Pensions for Canadians,* Minister of Supply and Services, Government of Canada, 1982, pp. 6-24.

9. See note 8 above.

10. *Report of the Royal Commission on the Status of Pensions in Ontario,* vol. 1, Government of Ontario, 1980, pp. 35-37.

11. President's Commission on Pension Policy, *An Interim Report,* Washington, D. C., 1980, p. 21.

12. Kotlikoff and Smith, p. 204.

13. Ibid., pp. 203-204.

14. Ibid., p. 204.

15. Ibid., p. 189.

16. See note 15 above.

17. Ibid., p. 191.

18. Ibid., p. 190.

19. Ibid., p. 215.

20. William Graebner, *A History of Retirement,* Yale University Press, New Haven and London, 1980, p. 133.

21. See note 20 above.

22. See note 20 above.

23. William C. Greenough and Francis P. King, *Pension Plans and Public Policy,* Columbia University Press, New York, 1976, p. 32.

24. Ibid., p. 33.

25. Graebner, p. 135.

26. Ibid., p. 155.

27. Greenough and King, p. 39.

28. See note 27 above.

29. Graebner, p. 153.

30. Ibid., p. 162.

31. Greenough and King, p. 72.

32. Graebner, p. 216.

33. See note 32 above.

34. See note 32 above.

35. Greenough and King, p. 61.

36. Ibid., pp. 61-62.

37. Ibid., p. 63.

38. Graebner, p. 218.

39. See note 38 above.

40. Greenough and King, p. 64.

41. Graebner, p. 218.

42. Kotlikoff and Smith, p. 28.

43. See note 42 above.

44. Greenough and King, p. 66.

45. Report of the Royal Commission, vol. 1, p. 46.

46. Ibid., p. 45.

47. See note 46 above.

48. Ibid., p. 44.

49. Ibid., p. 46.

50. Ibid., p. 47.

51. Charge of the Royal Commission on the Status of Pensions in Ontario, by Order-in-Council, O.C. 1098/77, dated April 20, 1977.

52. Interestingly, an arrangement very similar in concept to PURS was also proposed by the President's Commission on Pension Policy in the United States, appointed by President Carter during 1978-79.

53. *Report of the Royal Commission on the Status of Pensions in Ontario, Summary Report: A Plan for the Future,* Government of Ontario, 1981, p. 31.

54. Ibid., pp. 31-32.

55. Report of the Royal Commission on the Status of Pensions in Ontario, vol. 2, Government of Ontario, 1980, pp. 245-250.

56. U.S. Department of Labor data.

2

Work Life Perspective

In this chapter, we take the worker as the unit of analysis and concentrate on the characteristic dynamics of pension accumulation. The predictive period is the work life, parametrically specified in terms of a retirement age and the age of entry into an employment that is active at the beginning of the period. Benefit accumulation over this period may include several employments. In a probabilistic setting, we relate pension accrual to mobility, vesting rules, coverage or noncoverage of an employment by a pension plan, portability, plan characteristics and other variables.

We begin with a formalization of employment dynamics in Section 2.1 in terms of mobility, pension coverage and portability. Pension accrual is then projected onto this process, first in terms of pensionable service in Section 2.2. This section provides a preview of some of the concepts further structured in Section 2.3 in terms of pension benefits. An important development is the distinction between *pensionable service in the plan* and *work life pensionable service*. The framework for analyses of the impacts of partial coverage and portability is also established in this section.

The main section of the chapter, Section 2.3, is devoted to pension benefits. This section is organized in three parts. The first part (subsection 2.3.1) develops the benefit concepts and functions used in the ensuing analyses. These are introduced to measure *accrued benefits, termination benefits, "virtual" benefits,* and *work life benefits.* The third benefit concept is introduced to measure the expectation of a worker from the pension system as a whole, beyond his or her current employment. These functions are then used in the second part (subsections 2.3.2 through 2.3.5) to discuss a number of issues related to plan types, mobility, vesting rules, coverage and portability. In the third and final part of the chapter (subsection 2.3.6) we develop a methodology for the measurement of the extent to which pension expectations inhibit mobility. This section also uses the pension benefit concepts developed in subsection 2.3.1.

2.1 MOBILITY

The length of time a person spends in a given employment is subject to a high degree of variability. Most studies of manpower planning, including pensions, are based on a specific statistical characterization of this variability. The interest could be with a given position of employment, occupied by different incumbents, as in studies of recruitment and wastage or pension obligations in an organization. This is the firm or the plan perspective that we adopt in chapter 3. Or, the interest could be with a given individual, as he or she moves through different employments, as in studies of industrial mobility or pension accrual over several employments. This is the work life perspective of this chapter. In either case the lengths of employment will vary as the incumbent or the job changes.

Of all the factors that influence the duration of an employment, length of service to date and age of the employee are found to be the most important ones. Generally, the older the employee and/or the longer his or her tenure in the current employment, the less likely it is that he or she will terminate this employment. In reflection of these empirical facts, *termination rate schedules* used in actuarial studies have an age and a service dimension. In *fully select* schedules, dependency of termination rates on age and tenure is recognized for all age-tenure combinations. If the effect of tenure in itself is assumed away, so that termination rates vary only with age, the schedule is called *ultimate*. In the most common actuarial representation, the effect of tenure is recognized up to a certain attained age. Beyond this "select period," termination rates are assumed to depend on age only. Thus, most termination rate schedules used in actuarial work would have a select period of 5 to 10 years.

The term "termination rate" has a deterministic as opposed to a probabilistic connotation. In fact, "termination rate at age 50, tenure 10 is five percent" means that 5 percent of the 50 year old employees with 10 years of tenure will, on the average, terminate employment during the year. This is an ex post view of the employment termination process that disguises its probabilistic nature.

Alternatively, we may represent the length of employment of a given individual, ex ante, by a *random variable*. The law of variation could be described by a *probability distribution* that might, among other things, depend on age and tenure. This probability distribution could then be used to make statements about the length of employment of this individual, including probabilities of termination at different age-tenure positions.

These two seemingly different representations of employee mobility could be reconciled by a probabilistic interpretation of termination rates. In this interpretation, "termination rate at age 50, tenure 10 is five percent" is understood as a *conditional probability*. That is, *given* that an individual of entry age 40 remains 10 years on the job, the probability that he or she will terminate employment during the next year is 5 percent. With this interpretation, there is a one-to-one correspondence between termination rates applicable to an age and the probability distribution of the length of service for that age. When one is given, the other is also determined.

In addition to age and tenure, termination rates (or the corresponding probability distribution) may be regarded as dependent on other factors such as sex, race, employment status, savings, accrued pension, and so on. Economic and social influences, including industry characteristics, economic environment, availability and attractiveness of other job offers could also be considered. Clearly, the need to include one or more of these will be dictated by the objectives of a study. In our case, we shall confine our descriptions of employee mobility as it relates to age and tenure only, except in our discussions of the effects of limited pension coverage and portability. For latter purposes, we shall recognize the fact that the *existence* of a pension plan has an effect on termination rates (or length-of-stay distributions).

2.1.1 Termination Rates

Data that we report and discuss in the sequel on various pension-related measures are computed by way of either discrete or continuous mathematics. In the first case, employee mobility is represented by a fully select termination rate schedule. In the second case, the representation is in terms of a family of probability distributions. In either case the mobility data used are based on the actual experience of pension plan members.

The main data set is based on the turnover statistics of some large employee groups.[1] Some termination rates computed from this set are given in Table 2.1. In what follows, we refer to this particular schedule as the *moderate mobility schedule*. Two additional tables were developed from this schedule, one representing the *high* and the other the *low-mobility* sectors of the labor force. The high, moderate and low rates at each age and service point were in the ratios of 3:2:1, respectively. Thus while the moderate-mobility schedule is based on the actual experience of large employee groups that are covered by employment pension plans, the high and low-

TABLE 2.1. Actual and Fitted Termination Rates for Moderate Mobility Groups

Entry Age	Completed Length of Service						
	2	7	12	17	22	27	32
20	.200	.088	.056	.042	.036	.028	.022
	.199	.095	.048	.035	.032	.032	.032
25	.190	.084	.054	.040	.032	.026	.020
	.189	.089	.046	.035	.032	.032	.032
30	.180	.080	.052	.038	.030	.024	
	.179	.084	.045	.034	.032	.032	
35	.172	.076	.050	.046	.028		
	.171	.079	.043	.034	.032		
40	.164	.072	.048	.034			
	.163	.075	.042	.034			
45	.156	.068	.044				
	.156	.071	.041				
50	.148	.066					
	.149	.068					
55	.142						
	.140						

Top entries are empirical; they represent the actual experience of large groups of workers covered by pension plans.

TABLE 2.2. Mobility Measures

Entry Age	Prob. of Remaining in the Same Job until Retirement			Mean Length of Completed Employment (Yrs.)			Mean No. of Jobs Held to Retirement		
	Low	Mod-erate	High	Low	Mod-erate	High	Low	Mod-erate	High
20	.278	.075	.020	19.51	9.49	5.27	2.79	5.76	9.84
30	.350	.121	.042	17.58	9.63	5.80	2.39	4.50	7.27
40	.434	.190	.084	14.51	8.95	5.88	2.04	3.49	5.30
50	.538	.293	.161	10.17	7.14	5.18	1.72	2.62	3.67
60	.728	.526	.378	4.20	3.54	3.01	1.33	1.69	2.07

mobility schedules are normative. The high-mobility schedule implies a mean completed length of service of under 6 years (see Table 2.2) and approximates the mobility of the full work force in general. In what follows, we shall use this schedule to represent employee groups that are not covered by a pension plan.

The high, moderate and low mobility schedules specified above are used in two different forms in this book. Completed to 45×45 tables (from age at the beginning of the year 20 to 64) they provide the input for the discrete (annual) models of Chapter 3. This is in the mold of the traditional actuarial mathematics. The second form supports the continuous mathematics used for the computation of various examples in this chapter. For this purpose, a class of continuous probability distributions was fitted to each data set using appropriate statistical techniques. Termination rates as computed from these distributions are also given in Table 2.1. We note that although the fitted values are generally close to the actual rates, the differences are not negligible for some age-tenure combinations. This should be kept in mind in any comparison of the examples of this chapter with those of Chapter 3.

To provide the reader with an advanced feel of the various mobility assumptions used in the book, we present some measures in Table 2.2 that are computed from the three sets of data mentioned above. The first is the probability of remaining in the same employment until retirement, the second is the mean (or expected value)[2] of a completed employment,[3] and the third is the mean number of jobs held. All three measures are given for different ages of entry and assume a retirement age of 65.

2.1.2 Employment Dynamics

The employment patterns of individuals must be viewed in a more structured setting for some purposes. To examine the effects of limited pension coverage and portability, for example, it is necessary to use a covered/noncovered dichotomy. Thus an employee may be regarded as being in a covered or noncovered "state," respectively, depending on the coverage or noncoverage of his or her employment by a pension plan. As we will be primarily interested in lengths of time spent in the covered state, we will ignore unemployment, or equivalently for modeling purposes, regard it as noncovered employment. We will, however, distinguish as between mobility data applicable to covered and noncovered employments, either in terms of different termination rate schedules or in terms of different probability distributions of completed lengths of service.

This differentiation is not sufficient, however, to characterize employment dynamics for a study of pension coverage and portability. It is also necessary to specify how individuals move between noncovered and covered jobs and how they transfer their pension. Upon termination of a covered employment, an individual will move into another covered employment not with certainty but with a certain probability. (Or, equivalently, only a certain fraction of a group of similar individuals will, on termination of an employment covered by a pension plan, enter into another such employment). With the complement of this probability, the individual will start a noncovered employment or he or she will be unemployed. The same observations apply in the case of a noncovered employment; only in this case the transition probabilities involved may be different. (That is, the probability of moving from a covered to a noncovered employment, for example, may be different from the probability of moving from a noncovered to a noncovered employment.) Another uncertainty is created by the transferability of pension rights and assets between two covered employments. Thus upon termination of a covered employment, even if the next job is also covered, the pension rights and the underlying assets will be transferred (or transferable) in only a proportion of the times.

Consequently, in addition to lengths of stay in covered and noncovered jobs, these probabilities of transition and transfer must also be estimated or otherwise specified. They would be typical of the jobs that an individual is likely to encounter, depending on the industry and a number of other external factors. They would also depend on internal factors such as age and pension status of the individual. For example, other things being equal, we expect a decrease in an individual's propensity to make a transition from a covered to a noncovered employment as he or she approaches retirement. Clearly, inadequate pension accumulation to date would emphasize this tendency.

Technical aspects regarding the estimation and measurement of the probabilities in question are outside the scope of this book; however, as first approximations, the proportions of covered, noncovered, and portable employments in the industry involved may be used. These estimates can be improved by incorporating the expected lengths of stay in employments of different pension status. In the sequel we will use the following approach. Let c denote the probability that following and employment termination, an individual moves into a covered employment. This is the probability that we would like to estimate. Let us also denote by m_1 and m_2 the mean lengths of stay in covered and noncovered employments, respectively, as implied by applicable termination rates or length-of-stay distributions. Then, it can be shown that the ratio, $cm_1/[cm_1 + (1 - c)m_2]$, is the probability, in statistical equilibrium, that a randomly chosen employment in a work life is covered.[4] Under conditions approximating full employment, this probability should be nearly the same as the probability that a randomly chosen employment is covered. This latter probability is estimated by the proportion, say p, of covered employments in the industry or the opportunity set. If we then equate the above ratio to this coverage rate and solve for c, we find: $c = pm_2/[pm_2 + (1 - p)m_1]$. This expresses the probability of moving into a covered employment in terms of the expected lengths of stay in covered and noncovered employments and the coverage rate which are all easily observable. An inspection of this formula would show that c increases as p or m_2 increases but c decreases as m_1 increases. Also, $c = p$ if $m_1 = m_2$, $c = 1$ if $p = 1$, and $c = 0$ if $p = 0$, all as expected. The observation rate $c = p$ if $m_1 = m_2$ implies that the coverage rate is a reasonable approximation for the probability of moving into a covered employment, if the length of stay in an employment is independent of its pension coverage status. To the extent that the existence of pension coverage influences employee decisions to terminate employment, this estimate will be biased. The above formula improves on this by relating the probability in question to the mean lengths of stay in covered and noncovered jobs.

As a numerical example, suppose that the mean length of stay in a covered job is $m_1 = 6.5$ years and that in a noncovered job is $m_2 = 3.4$ years. These numbers follow from the moderate and high mobility data presented above, over a work life of 45 years, from age 20 to age 65. (The means given refer to a randomly chosen employment as opposed to mean lengths in Table 2.2 that refer to specific entry ages.) If the coverage rate in the industry is 25 percent, then, according to our formula, the probability is only about 15 percent that a transition will lead to a covered job. Also, the coverage rates of 50 and 75 percent imply transition probabilities of 34 and 61 percent, respectively.

Probabilities of transition and pension transfer, together with termination rates or length-of-stay distributions in covered and noncovered employments, provide a workable specification of employment dynamics as a framework for analyses of work life pension benefits and related issues.

2.1.3 Mobility and Pension Accrual

Following the employment termination process introduced above, suppose that the employment that is active at the start of our observations is covered by a pension plan. Upon termination of this employment, three different events of interest are possible: (1) the next job is also covered and the pension is portable; (2) the next job is covered but the pension is not portable; and (3) the next job is not covered. From the point of view of pension accrual, the first event is essentially, if not exactly, the same as the continuation of the previous employment. Thus covered and portable employments could be "lumped" together to form a continuous length of stay in the "covered state." The second event causes a transition from the covered state to itself whereby the employee starts counting from zero in terms of pension accrual. The third event causes a transition to the noncovered state where the employee may stay a length of time involving one or more employments (or unemployment).

If the employment at the start of our observations is not covered by a pension plan, then there are two follow-up events of relevance: (1) the next job is also not covered, and (2) the next job is covered by a pension plan. In the first case the spells of employment can be combined and viewed as a longer period of noncovered employment. The second case constitutes a transition to the covered state where pension accrual starts anew. Clearly, in either of these scenarios, the first employment could continue until retirement without any transitions.

In view of these observations, there are three types of interval that are of significance to pension accrual. The first starts in a covered state, includes one or more covered employments, all except the last one being portable, and terminates with a transition to another covered employment. The second is the same as the first except that it terminates with a transition to a noncovered employment. The third interval starts in a noncovered state, includes one or more noncovered employments, and terminates with a move to a covered employment. (Note that if the third type interval does not terminate with a transition to the covered state, it is of no relevance to pension accrual. Pension accrual takes place in the covered state over employment spells of the first two types.)

If we assume full coverage (i.e., all the employments in one's work life are covered by pension plans) and no portability, employment dynamics and pension accrual are both simplified. These conditions are approximated for some segments of the work force, such as in the automobile industry, where individuals move in and out of employments that are covered by similar or identical pension plans. In this case mobility affects pension accrual not in terms of lack of pension coverage or portability but in more subtle ways, through pension plan parameters and economic conditions. (Clearly such influences are also present under conditions of partial coverage and portability.) Important among these parameters and variables are the plan types, wage growth rates, inflation (or lack of indexation of benefits to inflation) and vesting rules. We will examine the influences of these elements on pension benefits and costs in some detail in the sequel. At this point, we would like to add the vesting rule to coverage and portability and note how mobility interacts with these elements in the accrual of creditable service.

Since vesting rules are usually expressed in terms of a prescribed minimum length of service or a combination of age and service, it is clear, as we noted before, that a stringent vesting requirement would have an adverse effect on pension accrual. Suppose, for example, that a person starts his or her working life at the age of 20 in an employment covered by a pension plan and retires from this employment at the age of 65. Clearly, no matter what the vesting rule might be, all of his or her 45 years of service would be pensionable. Consider a second, more mobile person over the same work life who changes employment at the age of 25, then at 31, again at 42, 46 and 56. Suppose that the third employment that starts at the age of 31 is not covered by a pension plan. Then, under the vesting rule of 10 years of service, only the fifth employment is creditable, resulting in a work life pensionable service of 10 years. If the vesting rule were to require 5 years of service, the individual would have been entitled to 30 years of pensionable service. Under full coverage, the work life pensionable service would have been 21 years under the vesting rule of 10 years of service, and 41 years under the vesting rule of 5 years of service. Also, even under the 10-year rule, total pensionable service would have been 21 years if the pension rights were transferred from the first to the second employment, and 34 years if all pensions were portable.

In these examples, we intentionally ignored the correlations that might exist between mobility and other variables, including vesting rules. It is true, as we suggested before, that the amount of pension loss suffered in a potential job change will be reduced in moving to a more liberal vesting rule. By reducing the reservation wage, however, this in turn might induce some individuals to be more mobile. And, since higher mobility means, in general, lower expected pensionable service, the amount of increase in work life pensionable service due to the application of a more liberal vesting rule may be overstated in the above examples. It should also be noted that in the absence of full coverage, it is not even clear that decreased mobility results in increased pension. Clearly, in our first example above, if the only job the individual held was not covered by a pension plan, there would not have been any accrual, meaning no mobility, no pension.

Other variables and parameters further complicate this situation. For one thing, the correspondence between pensionable service and pension benefits is not one-to-one. This relation depends on the pension plan type, the earnings base used in benefit calculations, wage growth, inflation, and many other factors. It may be that a shorter total pensionable service of a more mobile individual means a larger work life pension benefit than that related to a larger total pensionable service of a less mobile individual. This may be due, for example, to higher mobility during younger ages, when the value at retirement of accrued pension could be quite insignificant in the absence of inflation indexation, as against higher mobility during older ages when the period of erosion of benefits, from employment termination to retirement, is shorter. In what follows, we set out a comprehensive framework that is capable of accounting for these and other contingencies.

2.2 PENSIONABLE SERVICE

A proxy measure for pension benefit is the length of service during which this benefit accrues. By definition, such a length of service must meet the applicable vesting rule, and it is generally referred to as pensionable service.[5] Here we distinguish two measures of pensionable service: *pensionable service in the plan* and *work life pensionable service*. The first is the conventional concept that relates more naturally to employer perspective. It is also of interest and constitutes one of the building blocks of our methodology for work life perspective and it will be considered here. The second concept, that of work life pensionable service, has already been introduced by example in the previous section. It is of interest primarily from a work life perspective and as it relates to work life pension benefits.

As we have noted, the relationship between pensionable service and pension benefits may be complicated by a number of factors, including plan types and economic parameters. Also, longer pensionable service may not necessarily imply higher pension benefits. Lengths of pensionable service under two different scenarios can be compared in some respects, however, in much the same way as pension benefits, yielding similar conclusions. In such a situation the analysis should be based on pensionable service. For, as compared to pension benefits, considerations through pensionable service would be free from a number of economic parameters— such as the rates of return on investment and wage growth, the values of which must be assumed for the long term. This makes the analysis simpler, more precise and often more informative.

Pensionable service in the plan is a function of the period of employment, termination rates and the vesting rule. In subsection 2.2.1 we present a comparative examination of the alternative statutory vesting standards in terms of this measure—included are the ERISA and the 1986 Tax Reform Act standards. In subsection 2.2.2, we develop and discuss work life pensionable service, first under full coverage and then under partial coverage and portability. Although limited to pensionable service, this section anticipates the basic modeling approach and some of the developments throughout the rest of the book.

2.2.1 Pensionable Service in the Plan

Consider an individual who starts an employment covered by a pension plan at the age of t and expects to retire at age T. For ease of reference, we will denote his or her completed length of service in this employment by $X(t)$. *Ex ante,*$X(t)$ is a random variable characterized by termination rates applicable to entry age t. *Ex post,* it represents variations in the completed lengths of service of a group of similar individuals. In this latter context, we shall sometimes talk about an *age cohort* of individuals.

If it meets the vesting requirements of the plan, $X(t)$ is pensionable. For example, if the vesting rule calls for full vesting after at least s years of service, then $X(t)$ is pensionable if $X(t) \geqslant s$. If an age requirement must also be met, the $X(t)$ is pensionable if, in addition, $t + X(t) \geqslant \bar{t}$ where $\bar{t}$ is the minimum age requirement. We will assume that vesting requirements supercede eligibility requirements. The current statutory eligibility standards (age 25 and one year of service in the United States and one year of service in Canada) are met ahead of most vesting rules in practice.

ERISA Vesting Standards. As noted before, ERISA allows the sponsors of a pension plan to select one of three vesting provisions in satisfaction of the minimum vesting requirements. The first is full vesting after 10 years of service. The second is graded vesting that provides 25 percent vesting after five years of service which increases by 5 percentage points per year for the next five years and 10 percentage points per year for the next five years, thus resulting in full vesting after 15 years of service. The third is known as the Rule of 45. This alternative calls for 50 percent vesting after the earlier of 10 years of service or when the combination of service (minimum of five years) and the employee's age total 45. Thereafter, the employee's vested interest increases 10 percentage points per year for the next five years.

Generally, these provisions are regarded as equivalent. Differences in terms of pension costs among the three standards are attributed to actuarial assumptions and regarded as trivial. A choice between them could then be based on criteria other than cost, such as administrative simplicity and employee understanding.[6] Clearly, such considerations favor the first alternative. In fact, most pension plans have adopted the 10-year cliff vesting rule,[7] but not the other two. There are real differences between the ERISA vesting standards, however, differences that are not due to actuarial assumptions. The fact that termination rates generally decrease with tenure implies that the cliff-10 rule is the most stringent alternative for terminating employees and the least expensive in terms of plan costs.

The relationship between completed service and pensionable service under the three ERISA rules are shown in Table 2.3. In this table, X, rather than X(t), is used to denote a length of service, t the entry age, and T the retirement age. In addition to what has been noted above, some entries in this table also reflect the requirement under ERISA that an employee must be fully vested when he or she attains the normal retirement age, regardless of the vesting rules in effect, if the eligibility requirements are met. In addition, while a defined contribution plan may not use a maximum age for participation, a defined benefit plan may exclude those hired less than 5 years before the plan's normal retirement age. Thus with retirement at age 65, a person hired at the age of 58 will be fully vested in all cases, if he or she remains in this job until retirement. If the individual leaves a covered job at 64 after 6 years of service, however, he or she will be partially vested under the Rule of 45 or the graded vesting rule but will have no vested pension under the cliff vesting rule. We assume that beyond the entry age of 60 no pensionable service will accrue as the person will be excluded, even if he or she stays in the job until retirement. This assumption has no effect on the following analysis and conclusions.

Entries in Table 2.3 under the cliff vesting rule should be clear. To explain the graded vesting rule entries, note that this rule may result in full vesting for an employee who terminates before retirement, if he or she enters this employment more than 15 years before the age of retirement. In this case, a length of service of less than 5 years is not pensionable at all, but a length of service of at least 15 years is fully pensionable. In between these limits, vesting will be partial. If the length of service is greater than 5 but less than 10 years, then we have for the length of pensionable service:

$$[0.25 + 0.05(X - 5)]X = 0.05X^2.$$

Similarly, for $10 \leqslant X < 15$, we find that the pensionable service is:

$$[0.50 + 0.10(X - 10)]X = 0.10X^2 - 0.50X.$$

TABLE 2.3. Pensionable Service as a Function of Age at Entry (t) and Completed Service (X) under ERISA Vesting Standards

Age at Entry	Completed Service	Pensionable Service
1. Full Vesting after 10 Years of Service		
$t \leq T-10$	$X < 10$	0
	$X \geq 10$	X
$T-10 < t \leq T-5$	$X < T-t$	0
	$X = T-t$	X
$t > T-5$		0
2. Graded Vesting from 5 to 15 Years of Service		
$t \leq T-15$	$X < 5$	0
	$5 \leq X < 10$	$0.05X^2$
	$10 \leq X < 15$	$0.10X^2 - 0.50X$
	$X \geq 15$	X
$T-15 < t \leq T-10$	$X < 5$	0
	$5 \leq X < 10$	$0.05X^2$
	$10 \leq X < T-t$	$0.10X^2 - 0.50X$
	$X = T-t$	X
$t-10 < t \leq T-5$	$X < 5$	0
	$5 \leq X < T-t$	$0.05X^2$
	$X = T-t$	X
$T > T-5$		0
3. The Rule of 45		
$t \leq 25$	$X < 10$	0
	$10 \leq X < 15$	$0.10X^2 - 0.50X$
	$X \geq 15$	X
$25 < t \leq 35$	$X < (45-t)/2$	0
	$(45-t)/2 \leq X < (55-t)/2$	$0.10X^2 + (0.05t-1.75)X$
	$X \geq (55-t)/2$	X
$35 < t \leq T-10$	$X < 5$	0
	$5 \leq X < 10$	$0.10X^2$
	$X \geq 10$	X
$T-10 < t \leq T-5$	$X < 5$	0
	$5 \leq X < T-t$	$0.10X^2$
	$X = T-t$	X
$T > T-5$		0

T: Retirement age
T-5: Maximum entry age for participation

Other entries under graded vesting should now be clear.

For the Rule of 45, note that if $t \leqslant 25$, this rule reduces to graded vesting with 50 percent vesting after 10 years of service, increasing 10 percentage points per year for the next 5 years. For $t > 35$, the provision is again equivalent to graded vesting with 50 percent after 5 years, plus 10 percentage points per additional year. Note also that if $t > T - 10$, the provision cannot result in full vesting on any termination except retirement. The "Rule of 45" is really operational in the interval $25 < t \leqslant 35$. Here, if the length of service is less than half the difference between 45 and the age at entry, no vesting occurs. Graded vesting starts at this point with pensionable service computed as:

$$\{0.50 + 0.10 \ [X - (45 - t)/2]\}X = 0.10X^2 + (0.05t - 1.75)X.$$

Evidently, full vesting results after $(55 - t)/2$ years of service. As an example, suppose $t = 35$ and $X = 11$. According to the table, pensionable service is 11 years. This fact is the case, as after 5 years of service (age 40), age + service = 45 and a 50 percent vesting will result in 2.5 years of pensionable service. From this time on, percentage points applicable to the length of service will increase 10 per year, resulting in full vesting after 5 more years of service. Thus a length of service of 11 years is fully pensionable. As a second example, consider $t = 36$ and $X = 9$. Pensionable service from the table is 8.1 years. This also holds true, as in this case 50 percent of the length of service will be vested after 5 years of service, and 90 percent after 9 years of service. A minimum of 5 years of service is required under the Rule of 45 for 50 percent vesting, although age + service = 45 in this example only after 4.5 years of service.

Against this background, expected lengths of pensionable service can be computed and comparisons can be made among the three provisions. Comparative findings are presented in Table 2.4. This table ranks the ERISA provisions from the most liberal to the most stringent in terms of the expected pensionable service in the plan in different regions identified by the age of entry. The exact locations of the critical ages $t°$ and $t°°$ would depend on the applicable termination rates. According to the ranking given, if the entry age is less than $t°°$, which is between 25 and 35 years, graded vesting is the most liberal provision. After this age, the Rule of 45 is the most liberal in terms of the expected pensionable service in the plan. The cliff vesting provision is always dominated.

A rigorous proof of the ranking given in Table 2.4 requires the use of somewhat complicated mathematics that we choose to avoid in this book.[8] However, a partial justification can be provided as follows. First, if the entry age is 25 or less, both graded and cliff vesting rules are more liberal

TABLE 2.4. Rank of ERISA Vesting Provisions in Terms of Expected Pensionable
Service in the Plan as a Function of the Age at Entry (t)

t ≤ t*	t* ≤ t ≤ t**	t** < t
Graded	Graded	Rule of 45
Cliff Vesting	Rule of 45	Graded
Rule of 45	Cliff Vesting	Cliff Vesting

25 < t* ≤ t** < 35

than the Rule of 45 which results in only 5 pensionable years after 10 years
of service. On the other hand, if the entry age is not over $T-15$, which includes the above region, it can be shown mathematically that the expected
pensionable service is larger under ERISA graded vesting than under
ERISA cliff vesting, provided that termination rates decrease with
tenure.

Next, for entry ages that are more than 35 but not over $T-15$, it is clear
from Table 2.3 that the Rule of 45 is more liberal than cliff vesting. (It also
results in full vesting in 10 years in addition to yielding partial vesting after
only 5 years of service.) Also, as noted above, the converse is true for entry
ages 25 or less. It follows that a critical entry age exists between 25 and 35
before which cliff vesting and after which the Rule of 45 is more liberal.
This critical age is denoted by $t°$ in Table 2.4. Similarly, Table 2.3 shows
that the Rule of 45 is more liberal than graded vesting also after $t=35$.
Since the converse is true before $t=25$, it follows that there is another critical age, denoted by $t°°$, between 25 and 35, before which graded vesting
and after which Rule of 45 is more liberal. It can be shown mathematically
that both of these critical ages are unique and that $t°°$ is larger than $t°$.

For entry ages between $T-15$ and $T-10$, it is easy to see from Table 2.3
that Rule of 45 is more liberal than the other two provisions. Also, it can be
seen that the graded vesting rule compares more favorably with the cliff
vesting rule in this region than in $t \leqslant 25$. For entry ages over $T-10$, the
ranking in Table 2.4 is obvious.

To illustrate these findings we have computed the mean pensionable service in the plan for different entry ages under the alternative ERISA vesting standards. The results are shown in Table 2.5. The differences could be regarded as minor or significant depending on the precision of one's scale; however, they are not due to any restrictive assumptions. The only assumption made is that termination rates decrease with tenure, a well-established empirical fact. Even this assumption can be weakened somewhat so that termination rates may be increasing with tenure and the same conclusions follow.[9]

1986 Tax Reform Act Standards. Under the Tax Reform Act of 1986, all single-employer pension plans must meet one of the following two minimum vesting standards in order to qualify for tax benefits. The first is full vesting after 5 years of service. The second is a graded vesting provision that provides 20 percent vesting after 3 years of service, plus 20 percent per additional year, until full vesting in 7 years. Relationships between completed service and pensionable service under these rules are given in Table 2.6. Note that under graded vesting and for $3 \leqslant X \leqslant 7$, the pensionable service is given by:

$$[0.20 + 0.20 \ (X - 3)]X = 0.20X^2 - 0.40X.$$

TABLE 2.5. Expected Pensionable Service under ERISA Vesting Provisions

Age at Entry	Low Mobility			Moderate Mobility			High Mobility		
	Cliff 10	Graded	Rule of 45	Cliff 10	Graded	Rule of 45	Cliff 10	Graded	Rule of 45
20	17.86	18.01	17.68	7.34	7.54	7.18	3.10	3.29	2.98
30	16.03	16.16	16.23	7.56	7.75	7.79	3.66	3.84	3.85
40	13.05	13.17	13.65	6.94	7.11	7.67	3.76	3.94	4.42
50	8.79	8.90	9.37	5.19	5.35	5.91	3.09	3.26	3.77
t* :		27.39			27.32			27.25	
t**:		29.15			29.51			29.91	

TABLE 2.6. Pensionable Service as a Function of Age at Entry (t) and Completed Service (X) under the 1968 Tax Reform Act Vesting Standards

Age at Entry	Completed Service	Pensionable Service
1. Full Vesting after 5 Years of Service		
$t \leq T\text{-}5$	$X < 5$	0
	$X \geq 5$	X
$t > T\text{-}5$		0
2. Graded Vesting from 3 to 7 Years of Service		
$t \leq T\text{-}7$	$X < 3$	0
	$3 \leq X < 7$	$0.20X^2 - 0.40X$
	$X \geq 7$	X
$T\text{-}7 < t \leq T\text{-}5$	$X < 3$	0
	$3 \leq X < T\text{-}10$	$0.20X^2 - 0.40X$
	$X = T\text{-}t$	X
$T > T\text{-}5$		0

T: Retirement age
T-5: Maximum entry age for participation

We assumed, again, that a length of service that terminates with retirement is fully pensionable, subject only to the eligibility and exclusion provisions. The latter is represented by $t > T - 5$.

Using the relationships given in Table 2.6 and some graphical or mathematical analysis, it can be seen that the graded vesting rule is more liberal, in terms of expected values, than the cliff vesting rule. And this holds true for all entry ages provided that, given an entry age, termination rates decrease with tenure.[10] Some examples are given in Table 2.7. It is seen that in this case the differences are even less significant and the two rules may be considered equivalent for all practical purposes.

In addition to expected pensionable service in the plan, both ERISA and 1986 Tax Reform Act provisions can also be compared through the

TABLE 2.7. Expected Pensionable Service in the Plan under the 1986 Tax Reform
Act Vesting Standards

Entry Age	Low Mobility		Moderate Mobility		High Mobility	
	Cliff-5	Graded	Cliff-5	Graded	Cliff-5	Graded
20	18.75	18.83	8.35	8.47	3.97	4.09
30	16.89	16.95	8.56	8.67	4.56	4.68
40	13.86	13.93	7.93	8.04	4.68	4.80
50	9.57	9.63	6.17	6.27	4.03	4.15

variance of pensionable service. It turns out that, in both cases, graded
vesting rules result in less variability than cliff vesting rules. This result
should be intuitive, given the smoothing effects of a graded vesting provision that is built around a cliff vesting rule (i.e., 5 to 15 years for cliff-10; 3
to 7 years for cliff-5). Clearly this variance reducing effect adds more
meaning to the above rankings. Thus from an employee's point of view
moving from cliff vesting to graded vesting would both increase the expected value and decrease the variance of pensionable service in the plan.
From an employer's perspective this would imply higher but more predict-
able costs.

An examination of the results given in Tables 2.5 and 2.7, and the mean
length of service entries of Table 2.2 (which correspond to pensionable
service under full and immediate vesting), provides some insight into the
impact of mobility and vesting rules on the accrual of pensionable service
in an emplyment. While mobility has a very substantial impact, the influence of the vesting rule appears to be moderate. The reduction in expected pensionable service from full and immediate vesting (Table 2.2) to
cliff-5 rule, and from cliff-5 to cliff-10 rule is about one year in absolute
terms. As a relative reduction, this is marginal for the low-mobility sector
but significant for the high-mobility sector. On the other hand, for a given
vesting rule, there is a drastic reduction in qualifying service with increasing mobility.

This observation clearly ignores the possibility of any correlation between mobility and vesting rules. It could be argued on general grounds that vesting rules influence mobility. Indeed, delayed vesting is regarded as an instrument for the firm to reduce mobility; however, the observed insensitivity of pensionable service in the plan to the vesting rules weakens this argument. We shall come back to this point later in Section 2.3.

2.2.2 Work Life Pensionable Service—Full Coverage

In this section, we are interested in a characterization of the pensionable service for an individual (or a group of similar individuals) over a work life membership in pension plans. This characterization in terms of the mean and variance of the total pensionable service will serve a number of purposes. It will provide an introduction to the discussion of work life pension benefits later in the book. Technically, we shall see that pension benefit models of the next section are natural extensions of their pensionable service counterparts. Conceptually, as noted before, work life pensionable service may be a good proxy for the ultimate benefit to be derived from a work life membership in pension plans. Under the assumption that the pension is wage indexed (i.e., accrued at the same rate as the rate of growth of the average wage) total pensionable service at retirement can be regarded as pension benefits expressed as a fraction of the wage at retirement. Because this assumption does not hold in practice, we shall be concerned with the modeling and analysis of pension benefits separately in Section 2.3.

Consider an individual who starts a new employment covered by a pension plan at age t and expects to retire at age T. Assuming that all employments that he or she may hold during the time span from t to T are covered by a pension plan, what can we say about his or her total pensionable service?

At this point, in addition to full coverage, we further simplify the issue by assuming that the vesting rule is the same in all the employments that the individual may hold. This rule is represented by full vesting after s years of service. In numerical examples, we take s = 2, 5 and 10 which cover most of the recent and new statutory standards in the U.S. and Canada. Having looked at them in some detail above, in relation to pensionable service in the plan, we will ignore in what follows the graded vesting rules under ERISA and the 1986 Tax Reform Act.

It is important to note that the assumption of a uniform vesting rule that applies to all the employments in one's work life is not as restrictive as it might first appear. First, full coverage and uniform vesting rules are approximated in industries characterized by large unionized firms where competition and the collective bargaining process require high rates of coverage and similar or identical vesting rules. Second, since departures from statutory vesting standards could only be in the more liberal direction, work life pensionable service computed under a statutory rule will serve at least as a good lower bound. Third, in terms of expected values, results obtained under different vesting rules can be combined by taking a weighted average where the weights would reflect, for example, the prevalence of these different rules in the industry under consideration. Finally, the recent data indicate that the mean years until full vesting in all industries have been at or slightly below the statutory standard (i.e., 10 years during the post ERISA period).[11]

As before, we will assume that the eligibility requirement is satisfied when the vesting requirement is satisfied. The maximum age for exclusion for membership in a (defined benefit) plan will be taken as $T - e$, relative to the retirement age T. At the present time, $e = 5$ (years) in the U.S. and $e = 1$ in federal and most provincial plans in Canada. These numbers are used in some numerical examples below.

Under these specifications, mean, variance and other statistical measures for work life pensionable service can be developed by mathematical means. The representations are somewhat complicated, however, and we will only sketch out the conceptual framework.[12]

The employment taken at age t may last until retirement. It will then be pensionable provided the length, $T-t$, of the work life is larger than the service requirement for vesting, s. The probability of this event (that the first job lasts until T) is computable from termination rates or length-of-stay distributions. If the first job terminates before retirement with a length of service of u, it will be pensionable if $u \geqslant s$ but not if $u < s$. In any case, at the point of termination of the first job (at age $t+u$) the individual will be at the start of a new employment. Under the model assumptions, this employment will also be covered by a pension plan of the same vesting rule. Therefore, the process that started at age t will resume in a cycle. The entry age will be $t + u$, rather than t, and the length of the work life will be $T - (t + u)$ rather than $T - t$. This process will continue, in a recurrent fashion, with the durations of successive employments being governed by termination rates or probability distributions. If we thus consider all possible employment patterns and their probabilities, the weighted average of total lengths of pensionable service associated with these patterns will be the mean pensionable service. Variance and other measures can also be developed by using the same recurrent structure.

Some examples computed from formulae derived on the basis of this methodology are given in Table 2.8. One observation of some importance to later developments is that as opposed to pensionable service in a given employment, work life pensionable service is substantially affected by the vesting provisions. As noted before, with an expected length of employment of between 5 and 6 years for most ages of entry (Table 2.2), our high-mobility scenario approximates the mobility of the full-time work force in

TABLE 2.8. Mean Work Life Pensionable Service under Different Cliff Vesting Rules[1]

From Age[2]	Low Mobility			Moderate Mobility			High Mobility		
	10	5	2	10	5	2	10	5	2
20	40.69	42.89	44.52	34.09	38.96	43.42	26.80	33.79	41.69
30	31.42	33.24	34.61	26.43	30.27	33.81	21.03	26.39	32.50
40	22.04	23.53	24.68	18.38	21.28	24.08	14.67	18.56	23.18
50	12.58	13.73	14.75	10.15	12.13	14.33	7.97	10.40	13.75
60	3.11	3.64	4.81	2.18	2.63	4.57	1.66	1.89	4.31

[1] An employment that terminates with retirement is regarded as pensionable, irrespective of the vesting rule, if the employee is not excluded from membership in the plan. Exclusion is assumed beyond the entry age of 60 under the cliff-10 and cliff-5 rules.
[2] The accumulation period is from the age given to retirement at 65.

the U.S. and Canada. Evidently, this level of mobility is heavily penalized by a vesting rule that requires 10 years of service. At the other extreme, the low-mobility sector appears unaffected by the vesting rule. Also of interest are the results under the moderate scenario, as this represents the mobility patterns of employee groups covered by pension plans. Here too, the vesting rule has a substantial impact in determining work life pensionable service.

If, under a specific vesting rule, a group of similar individuals exhibit a job mobility pattern that is similar to one of our three scenarios, what would the average work life pensionable service be under this rule? Table 2.8 addresses this question. It is tempting to use these results also to estimate the consequences of a given change in the vesting rule. This should be done with some care, however, because the model used to compute the above table does not take into explicit account the possible effects of delayed vesting on job mobility.

Mathematical analysis not reported here shows that the rate of change in expected work life pensionable service in response to a change in the vesting rule is proportional to the expected number of jobs held from the beginning of the work life to age $T - s$. The latter represents both the age beyond which an employment is not pensionable under the vesting rule of s years of service and the maximum age for participation. Thus the loss or gain in work life pensionable service, induced by a unit increase or decrease in the service requirement for vesting, can be approximated by multiplying this number by the marginal change in pensionable service in a typical employment. As mobility increases, so does the number of different employments held. Therefore, the marginal change in work life pensionable service is larger in the higher mobility sectors. Evidently, the impact of mobility is magnified as it pertains to work life pensionable service. On the other hand, this effect may not be as strong with regard to pensionable service in any one employment. This is clear from a comparison of the numerical results we reported so far for pensionable service in an employment and work life pensionable service.

2.2.3 Work Life Pensionable Service—Partial Coverage and Portability

We now extend the discussion of work life pensionable service to partial coverage and portability. Evidently, questions related to pensionable service under conditions of limited coverage and portability are of interest in the context of a pension system in an industry or an employment category.

From continuous employment and full pension coverage to partial coverage and portability, there is a significant degree of complication in the characterization and measurement of work life pensionable service. Here our characterization will be based on the employment dynamics described in Section 2.1.2 and, again, we will not dwell on mathematical developments.[13.] Recall the distinction between covered and noncovered employments in terms of termination rates or length of stay distributions. Also a probability measure, c, was developed in Section 2.1.2 in terms of the coverage rate p and mean lengths of stay in covered and noncovered employments. This measure represented the probability of moving into a covered job following an employment termination. By implication $1 - c$ was the probability of entering a noncovered employment or unemployment. Likewise, upon termination of a covered employment, if the next job was also covered, pension rights and underlying assets could be transferred with a certain probability. We denote this probability by π. In a first approximation, π could be taken as the proportion of employments with portable pensions that the group of individuals under study are likely to encounter. The initial conditions are specified in terms of age, tenure in the current employment, and the pension status of this employment as being covered or noncovered.

In our discussion in Section 2.1.3 of mobility and pension accrual, we identified three types of employment intervals. Two of these were employment spells in covered jobs that involved transfers; one terminated with retirement or a transition to a covered but not portable job, the other with retirement or a move to a noncovered job or unemployment. The third was a length of stay in the noncovered "state" that eventually terminated with retirement or a transition to the covered "state."

Suppose that the first employment is covered by a pension plan so that the individual is in the covered state at the beginning of his or her work life at age t. This would represent the start of a type 1 or a type 2 interval. For simplicity, we retain the assumption that a new job is taken at age t. This assumption will be dropped later in discussing pension benefits to examine the impact of tenure in the current job. Upon termination of this employment with a completed length of service of say $X(t)$, the individual will move: (1) either into a covered employment with a pension transfer, with probability $c\pi$; (2) or into a covered employment without a transfer, with probability $c(1 - \pi)$; (3) or into a noncovered employment, with probability $1 - c$. In all cases, $X(t)$, as a random variable will be governed by the applicable termination rate schedule or the probability distribution. In the second or third cases, the type 1 interval of pension accrual (referred to above) would terminate with the employment in question. It will be pensionable if $X(t) \geqslant s$, not pensionable if $X(t) < s$. Following the transition, the pension accumulation process would resume over a work life of length $T - t - X(t)$ with the initial state being covered in case 2 or not covered in case 3. Provided it is pensionable, $X(t)$ will be added to any future accruals over this period. In the first case, $X(t)$ will be added to the length of service in the second employment. At the time of termination of the latter, the situation will repeat itself by way of the same three transitions. Eventually, either retirement or a transition of the second or third nature will result in an assessment of the total time spent in the covered state. If this total time is pensionable, it will be added to any future creditable service. If not, it will be lost for pension purposes. The process again will resume either in the covered or the noncovered state with a corresponding reduction in the length of the work life. Ultimately, the accumulation process will terminate with retirement.

The framework briefly described in the above paragraph has been developed in detail in terms of a number of mathematical functions.[14] Some examples computed from the expected value function are given by Figures 2.1 and 2.2. These examples assume a work life of 45 years, extending from age 20 to age 65, with the first job not covered. The transition probability c is related to the coverage rate p in accordance with the formula given in Section 2.1.2 which takes into account the mean lengths of service in covered and noncovered employments. This relationship is shown as an insert to Figure 2.1. Note that c is increasing in p at a decreasing rate. This is due to the assumption that the mean length of service in a covered job is

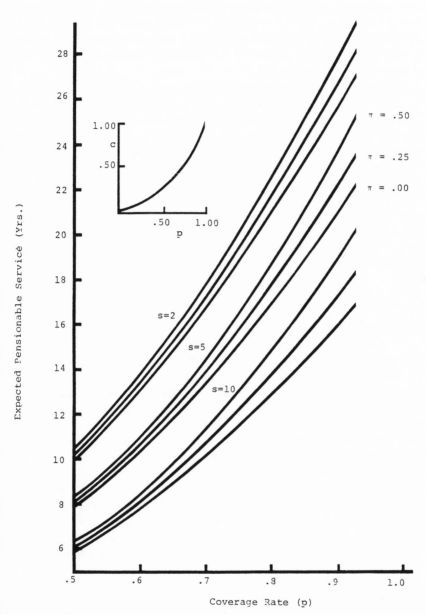

Figure 2.1 Expected work life (20 to 65) pensionable service as a function of the coverage rate (p) under different portability (π) and vesting rules (s)

longer than the mean length of service in a noncovered job. If such is the case, probability of moving into a covered job must be less than the proportion of covered jobs (the coverage rate) in the industry under consideration. The length of stay distributions in covered and noncovered employments were represented by our moderate and high mobility data, respectively.

The message from these results is very clear. While the coverage rate has a substantial impact on work life pensionable service, portability means very little under low to moderate rates of coverage. Ability to transfer pension rights, irrespective of the vesting status, is meaningful only under high rates of coverage and stringent vesting rules. We shall see later that these effects and conclusions are somewhat modified in passing from pensionable service to pension benefits, especially in the case of final earnings plans. Note also that the expected pensionable service out of a career of 45 years is never more than 28.2 years (Figure 2.1), although up to 90 percent of the jobs are covered by a pension plan and half of these are portable. This is due to the above noted nonlinear relationship between the coverage rate p and the probability of moving into a covered employment c. For p = 0.90, for example, we have c = 0.78.

2.3 PENSION BENEFITS

Because of the existence in practice of a variety of pension plan types and the fact that termination benefits are not indexed to wage or inflation, work life pensionable service is not a good proxy for work life pension benefits. For the same reasons, the impact of mobility on pension benefits may be more critical than its impact on pensionable service.

In this section, again by taking the individual as the unit of analysis, we concentrate on the accumulation of pension benefits during a work life as it varies with mobility, plan types, vesting rules, coverage and portability. The analyses are in terms of three different functions that are introduced in Section 2.3.1. The first of these is the *accrued benefit* function. It corresponds to traditional benefit formulae that convert pensionable service to pension benefits under different plan types. The second is the *termination benefit function*. It measures the expected pension benefit for the currently active employment of a given individual. Individuals are parametrized in terms of entry age to the current employment, tenure in this employment, and retirement age. Other parameters, such as gender, accrued pension to date, are also possible. The third function is called the *virtual benefit* function. It represents the expected pension benefits related to employments, if any, that are taken from the time of termination of the current employment to the time of retirement. This concept is introduced

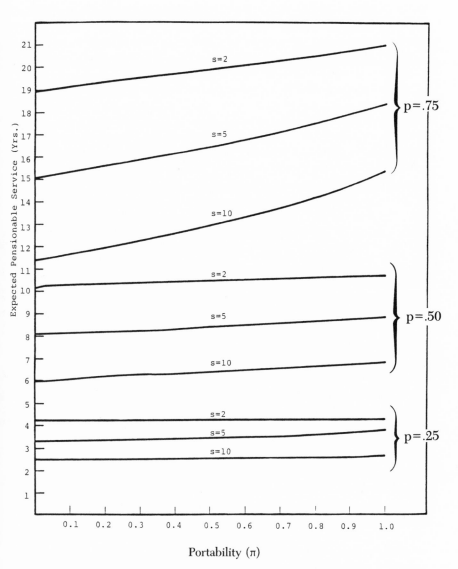

Figure 2.2 Expected work life (20 to 65) pensionable service as a function of portability (π) under different coverage rates (p) and vesting rules (s)

to measure the expectation of an individual from the pension system beyond his or her current job.

These functions are used in the sequel to investigate the impacts of plan types (2.3.2), mobility (2.3.3) and vesting rules (2.3.4) on benefit accumulation. They are also used in subsection 2.3.6 to measure the extent to which pension expectations inhibit mobility. The discussion of partial coverage and portability is extended from work life pensionable service to work life pension benefits in subsection 2.3.5.

Also emphasized in this section is the measurement issue. In an attempt to relate the value of pension benefits to their purchasing power at retirement as well as to the current economic status of the worker, we express pension benefits both as *replacement rates* at retirement and *reservation rates* over the period of accrual. The first is the conventional valuation by which pension benefits are expressed as a fraction of the wage at retirement. It brings into focus the adequacy of pension benefits at the beginning of the postretirement period. As a complementary method of valuation, we also use the concept of reservation rate. This is the fraction of wage, during the period of pension accrual, the invested value of which would buy the accrued pension at retirement.

Types of pension plans used in the following applications and data on their structural characteristics are based on recent survey results[15] as summarized in Chapter 1. According to these results, defined benefit plans in the United States cover 73.5 percent of plan participants with an average of 210 participants per plan, while defined contribution plans account for 24.7 percent of the covered population with an average of 34 per plan. The latter group is represented below by a money purchase plan. In the defined benefit category, we have chosen the career average plan and final average plans with averaging periods of 3, 5 and 10 years. This covers almost all the unit benefit plan types in use in practice.

A significant class of plans not explicitly included in the following is the flat benefit group. Most of these plans relate benefit to length of service. Sometimes referred to as unit credit flat benefit (UCFB) plans, these provide a fixed benefit amount for each year of pensionable service, payable on reaching the retirement age. In addition to recognizing the length of service, this design also relates benefits to earnings growth. Through periodic employee-employer negotiations, the annual credit is updated in recognition of the growth in wages, so that the final retirement benefit generally reflects the wage history. Depending on the frequency and retroactivity of the negotiated increases in benefit, patterns of benefit accrual in UCFM plans would be similar in practice to career average or final earnings plans. If negotiated increases in flat benefits parallel the growth in earnings, a UCFB plan would effectively operate as a career average plan. However, UCFB plans usually update previously accrued benefits with the additional objective of maintaining the real value of past accrued benefits of active employees. In this respect, benefits accruing under a UCFB plan would be more comparable to that under a final average plan. With this interpretation of flat benefit plans, the four defined benefit plans selected and the money purchase plan make up a representative set.

In terms of economic assumptions, the illustrations below are based on an inflation rate of 5 percent, a real rate of return of 2.5 percent, and a real wage growth rate of 2 percent. These assumptions are consistent with long-term trends. They were arrived at by means of simulation runs based on the accrued benefit formula under different plan types. They represent a set of assumptions that produce nearly the same replacement rates at retirement, following a work life of 35 years, as those based on recent empirical studies.[16] In addition to this limited calibration of the models, sensitivities of some of the more critical results to variations in economic assumptions are also analyzed. On the conceptual side, all benefit calculations are based on the assumption that the impact of inflation is fully reflected in wages and that the real interest rate is unaffected by inflation. That is, wages grow at a rate equal to the sum of inflation and real wage growth rates, and the interest rate increases with inflation.

It is important to note at this point that the various benefit measures introduced above are not adjusted for mortality. The reason is that in this chapter pension costs are of no concern to us. If an individual survives to postretirement years, he or she may receive some benefits; we are interested in an analysis of these. If the person dies before retirement, the work life will also terminate and the benefit accrual will stop. In this sense, the length of the work life may appear to be not fixed (i.e., from age 20 to age 65) but variable. But in this case, the pension benefit due at retirement, however measured, is not meaningful, for it will not be received by the individual. From the perspective of a work life, mortality considerations would be relevant only in relation to death and survivors benefits, topics that are outside our scope. On the other hand, mortality will play an important role in our discussions in Chapter 3 of pension costs from the plan perspective.

2.3.1 Models and Functions

As an extension of the methodology outlined in Section 2.2, we now introduce three basic functions that fully characterize expected pension benefits. For this purpose, the period of benefit accumulation is specified, as before, as the interval from age t to age T of continuous employment. (Allowances for partial coverage and unemployment are made in Section 2.3.6). Parameter T is the age of retirement or the end of the predictive period, and t is the age of entry into a new employment. This employment is referred to as the *current employment.* In this section, we add a third time parameter, denoted by y, to represent tenure in the current employment. Thus, the attained age of the employee is t + y. By varying the triplet, t, y and T, we will be able to examine the influences of age, tenure in the current employment and the retirement age.

Implicit in the above representation is the division of the period from age t to age T into two parts: the interval from age t to age t + y which has been observed; and the interval from age t + y to age T which represents the future. Over these intervals, the concern is with "age-tenure cohorts (t,y)," for varying t and y, meaning individuals of tenure y in their current employments to which they had entered at age t. For such cohorts, we introduce the following concepts of pension benefit: (1) *accrued benefit* in the current employment during (t,t+y); (2) *termination benefit* of current employment, including accrued benefit; and (3) cumulative benefit from termination of current employment to time T. We call the third benefit the *virtual benefit* of cohort (t,y) as it is not associated with actual employment. It only reflects the expectation of the cohort from the pension system beyond the current job. Note that the accrued benefit is deterministic while termination and virtual benefits are random variables. We will call the sum of termination and virtual benefits the *work life benefit* during (t,T).

Accrued Benefit. It will be convenient to parametrize the accrued benefit function in terms of the time of entry into an employment as measured backward from T. Thus the accrued benefit of cohort (t,y) will be denoted by $B(T-t,y)$, with reference to the current employment of length y that started $T-t$ time units *before* retirement. Similarly, we denote by $W(x)$ the wage at x time units *before* retirement. $W(T-t)$, for example, would be the wage at the time of entry into the current employment and $W(0)$ the wage at retirement. We take the wage function as given and normalized such that $W(0) = 1$. This is for the representation of pension benefits as a replacement rate at retirement.

Accrued pension would also depend on the plan type and the vesting rule. In terms of defined benefit plans, we consider flat benefit (FB), career average (CA), final wage (FW) and final average (FA) plans. We also consider defined contribution, money purchase (MP) plans. The vesting rule is represented by a service requirement of s years. For simplicity we assume a maximum entry age for eligibility of $T-s$. This amounts to the requirement that in order to be pensionable all the employments, including the one that terminates with retirement, should meet the vesting rule.

Clearly, $B(T-t,y) = 0$ for y < s. For y ⩾ s, the specific form of the accrued benefit function would depend on the plan type. In the simplest case, for flat benefit plans, we have $B(T-t,y) = fy$, where f is the flat benefit amount per year of pensionable service. As a second example, for final wage plans the relationship is: $B(T-t,y) = lyW(T-t-y)$ where l is the benefit level expressed as a percentage of wage. Recall that $W(T-t-y)$ represents the wage $T-t-y$ time units before retirement. Since this corresponds to age $t+y$, the attained age, the accrued benefit is calculated as a percentage of the current wage. Expressions can also be developed for career-average plans, final average plans of various averaging periods, and for money purchase plans.[17]

Termination Benefit. The termination benefit function of cohort (t,y) will be denoted by $\bar{B}(t,y)$. This includes the accrued benefit, if any, as of age $t+y$, and the future benefit from $t+y$ to the age at which the current employment is terminated. This future benefit and therefore the entire termination benefit $\bar{B}(t,y)$ will be regarded as random. In this chapter, we shall be concerned mostly with its expected value. We shall refer to this measure as the *expected termination benefit* or as the *mean termination benefit* with respect to an individual or with respect to a cohort of similar individuals—i.e., "age-tenure cohort (t,y)."

A framework for the characterization of $\bar{B}(t,y)$ as a random variable is as follows. First, having started at age t (i.e., $T-t$ years before retirement) and having lasted y years, the current employment may extend to retirement, resulting in the benefit $B(T-t, T-t)$. The probability of this event is the probability that, given that it lasted y years, an employment taken at age t will last $T-t$ years; this can be computed from termination rates or the probability distribution of employment durations. Note that $B(T-t, T-t)$ represents accrued benefit corresponding to an employment of length $T-t$ (second argument) taken $T-t$ years before retirement (first argument). Second, if the current employment terminates before retirement with length u, then $B(T-t,u)$ will accrue on termination, provided that $u \geqslant s$. The probability that, having lasted y years, the current employment will terminate at age $t+u$ (tenure $y+u$) can again be computed from mobility data for any u. These representations easily result in mathematical expressions for the mean and other statistical measures related to the termination benefit of cohort (t,y).[18]

It should be noted that the time frame of this representation is somewhat more complicated than that of Section 2.2 mainly because of the inclusion of tenure in the current employment as an additional parameter. With this, the beginning of our observations is not necessarily coincident with the start of a new employment, and thus the job renewal process does not start with a "complete" interval, unless $y=0$. Rather, the first interval is the residual tenure in the current employment. Also, on taking $y=0$ and $B(T-t,u)=u$, the concept of termination benefit is seen to include that of pensionable service in the plan of the previous section.

Virtual and Work Life Benefits. The virtual benefit function of cohort (t,y), to accrue from all subsequent employments, following the termina-

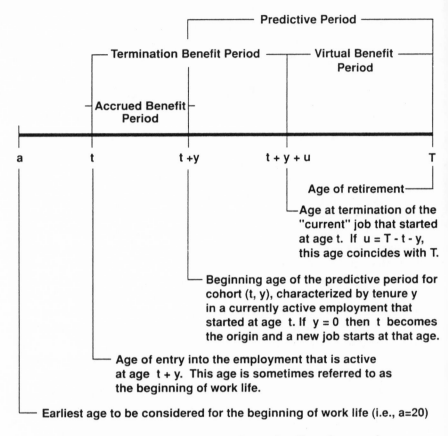

Figure 2.3 Time parameters and periods of benefit accrual

tion of the current employment, will be denoted by $\bar{B}(t,y)$. If the current employment terminates at age $t+y+u$, for some u, then the period of accumulation for $\bar{B}(t,y)$ will be from age $t+y+u$ to age T. (See Figure 2.3)

As a background for the derivation of mathematical expressions for the mean, variance, etc. of the virtual benefit of cohort (t,y), note first that $\tilde{B}(t,y) = 0$ if the current employment extends to retirement or if it terminates less than s years before retirement. On the other hand, the benefit $B(u,u)$ would accrue if: (1) there is an employment termination at u years before retirement; (2) the *following employment* lasts until retirement; and (3) $u \geqslant s$. If the *following employment* in (2) above terminates before retirement with length $x < u$, then $B(u,x)$ would accrue, provided that $x \geqslant s$. Probabilities of these events can be computed from mobility data; however, the developments are rather complicated because of the implicit inclusion of several employments during the period of accrual of virtual benefits.[19]

The work life benefit function is defined as the sum of termination and virtual benefits and is denoted by $B°(t,y)$. Thus $B°(t,y) = \bar{B}(t,y) + \tilde{B}(t,y)$. This extends the concept of work life pensionable service of the previous section in a two-component structure that will serve a number of purposes in the sequel.

2.3.2 Plan Types and Benefits

A balanced discussion of the virtues and limitations of different pension plan types would have to take into account the perspectives of different economic agents. In this subsection, we confine our attention to the existence and value of pension benefits from the point of view of employees. This discussion will be extended in Chapter 3 to the magnitude and predictability of pension costs as matters of concern to employers.

From an employee's perspective, important factors in assessing a pension plan type include inflation, risk, and comparability with current economic status. First, pension benefits under career average plans deteriorate rapidly with inflation, as the accrual of pension is based on past wages. The prospects are somewhat better in final average plans where, although benefits related to previous employments also erode rapidly with inflation, current job benefits would exhibit a good follow-up. On the other hand, accrued benefits are fully protected from inflation in money purchase plans in which both past and current benefits increase with interest rates reflecting inflation. Second, and substantially for the same reason, defined benefit plans, especially career average plans, do not yield "age-neutral" benefits. For over comparable employment durations, termination benefits of younger workers are lower in value than those of older workers. Moreover, since deferred annuity is cheaper the longer the deferral period, contributions of younger employees may buy much of, even more than, the benefits promised on the basis of their service in contributory defined benefit plans. In contrast, money purchase plans are "age-neutral" in the sense that the employer contributes a fixed percentage of employee earnings and the same fraction of salary is paid by every age cohort in contributory plans. This does not mean, however, that pension benefits accruing from a pensionable service would depend only on its length, not on its timing. Age-related benefit differentials would prevail in money purchase plans also, depending on the decrease in termination rates with age, as well as on economic conditions.

In addition to being sensitive to inflation, pension benefits under career average plans are not well related to current economic status of the worker, for wages grow but past benefits do not. This relationship is improved under final earnings and money purchase plans where, in the former, current job benefits are better related to final earnings. Also, in relation to other forms of saving, comparative value of benefits in career average plans is difficult to ascertain for the average worker, as such a comparison involves annuities. This difficulty is compounded in final earnings plans because of wage growth in the current job. In money purchase plans, on the other hand, accrued benefits are readily comparable with other assets.

In spite of these shortcomings, defined benefit plans are dominant in practice, mainly due to the fact that they promise a fixed benefit rate, not a fixed contribution rate as in money purchase plans. This makes it possible for individuals to spread the risk of benefit losses over their work lives, rather than to concentrate this risk around the time of retirement. Even if a defined contribution pension account holds a low-risk diversified portfolio, it is possible that a significant loss will be realized during the time of retirement of a given age cohort, due to a sharp decline in security prices. Such a decline took place in November 1987, for example, with dire consequences for retirees during late 1987 and early 1988. The defined benefit scheme avoids this problem by its well known risk-spreading feature which involves investing primarily in long-term securities. Suppose, for example, that a defined benefit pension fund takes the deposits and invests them in long-term bonds. The fund experiences capital gains during periods of lower-than-expected inflation and losses during periods of higher-than-expected inflation. Given the long-term horizon, these gains and losses cancel out over several age cohorts, however, leaving the fund with almost no long-term risk. This in turn makes it feasible to "define" one's benefit well ahead of time.

As a second relative advantage of defined benefit plans, it could be argued that defined contribution plans create a *selectivity problem*.[20] While defined benefit plans offer only annuities, most defined contribution plans offer a lump sum option. The problem arises in the second case as follows. Retirees expecting earlier death choose lump sums, while those expecting unusual longevity choose annuities; however, retirees expecting average longevity are worse off with either choice than they would have been under a defined benefit plan. If they choose annuities, they will get less because of overcompensation for super longevity prospects. If they choose lump sums, they will consume less to protect against super longevity. In defined benefit plans, on the other hand, there is no lump sum option, workers are committed to annuities early, and fair annuity prices can be set to ensure that the aggregate consumption approximates the collective pension value. This in turn creates a subsidy problem, however, as retirees who live long will receive more than those who die early.

There are a number of other points that can be made in a discussion of the relative advantages and disadvantages of defined benefit versus defined contribution plans. However, the two overriding considerations are the risk-spreading characteristics of defined benefit plans against the erosion of pension benefits under these arrangements from employment termination to retirement. If termination benefits were indexed to inflation, a final-earnings defined benefit plan would certainly be the most desirable plan type from the workers' perspective. Postemployment indexation of pension benefits is not a common practice, however. Another remedial measure is the provision of an option for an employee to switch from a defined benefit to a money purchase mode at the time of employment termination. This application is also uncommon in practice, but it may increase in popularity in the future.

We now turn to a systematic examination of how pension benefits evolve over work life for different cohorts in different plans. As instruments, we use the benefit functions introduced earlier. These relate to: (1) the accrued benefit of age-tenure cohort (t,y) in a currently active employment of length y that started at age t; (2) the mean termination benefit of cohort (t,y) on termination of the current employment; and (3) the mean virtual benefit beyond the current employment. These benefits are expressed both as replacement rates at retirement and reservation rates over the period of accrual. The first method of measurement simply implies a scaling of the wage function so that the wage at retirement is unity.

Conversion from replacement rates to reservation rates is achieved as follows. Consider, for example, the mean termination benefit, expressed as a replacement rate, of cohort (t,y), induced by a career-average plan of one percent benefit level. Denote this benefit by $\bar{M}_{CA}(t,y)$. Consider next the mean termination benefit, similarly defined, but this time induced by a money purchase plan of one percent contribution level *under full and immediate vesting*. Denote this benefit by $\bar{M}^{\circ}_{MP}(t,y)$. The ratio, $R_{CA}(t,y) = M_{CA}(T,Y)/\bar{M}^{\circ}_{MP}(t,y)$ would then be the contribution level needed in the money purchase plan to but the same annuity at retirement as that implied by a career average plan of one percent benefit level. As defined, $\bar{M}^{\circ}_{MP}(t,y)$ is the invested value at retirement of one percent of the wages received from the current employment. Thus, with respect to his or her retirement income, a worker should be indifferent in the mean, under reasonable assumptions, as between the career average plan in question and a wage increase of $R_{CA}(t,y)$ percent. This we call the reservation rate version of $\bar{M}_{CA}(t,y)$. Definitions for other benefits and plans are similar.

Some examples are presented in Table 2.9, Table 2.10 and Table 2.11, using a retirement age of 65. Defined benefit plans assume a one percent benefit level and the money purchase plan assumes a one percent contribution level. Results for other benefit and contribution levels can be

TABLE 2.9. Accrued Benefits in Different Plans as Replacement and Reservation Rates (Moderate Mobility, Cliff-5 Vesting Rule)

| Entry | | Money Pur. | | Career Ave. | | Final Average | | | | | |
| | | | | | | 10 Years | | 5 Years | | 3 Years | |
Age	Tenure	Rep.	Res.	Rep.	Res.	Rep.	Res.	Rep.	Res.	Rep.	Res.
20	10	1.30	1.00	0.60	0.46	0.60	0.46	0.70	0.53	0.75	0.57
	20	2.54	1.00	1.81	0.71	2.42	0.95	2.85	1.12	3.05	1.20
	30	3.71	1.00	4.28	1.15	7.40	1.99	8.70	2.34	9.31	2.50
	40	4.83	1.00	9.30	1.93	20.08	4.16	23.60	4.89	25.26	5.23
30	10	1.24	1.00	1.21	0.98	1.21	0.98	1.42	1.15	1.52	1.23
	20	2.41	1.00	3.68	1.53	4.93	2.04	5.80	2.40	6.21	2.57
	30	3.52	1.00	8.70	2.47	15.06	4.27	17.70	5.02	18.94	5.37
40	10	1.17	1.00	2.47	2.10	2.47	2.10	2.90	2.47	3.10	2.64
	20	2.29	1.00	7.49	3.28	10.04	4.39	11.80	5.16	12.63	5.52
50	10	1.11	1.00	5.02	4.51	5.02	4.51	5.90	5.30	6.31	5.67

readily obtained by multiplying the corresponding entries with the level desired. Note, however, that while a one percent benefit level in defined benefit plans is not much lower than the average benefit level in practice, a one percent contribution level in the defined contribution plan is much below the range used in applications for primary pension plans. Rather than choosing an arbitrary benefit or contribution level, we give the results for levels of unity for ease of extrapolation. For this reason, defined benefit plans are comparable in absolute terms only among themselves, not with the money purchase plan. All computations are based on a 5-year cliff vesting rule and the moderate mobility assumption.

Accrued benefits are given in Table 2.9 for selected cohorts. As an example, consider an individual who has 20 years on a covered job that he or she started at age 30—i.e., cohort (30,20). Under a career average plan (of one

TABLE 2.10. Expected Termination Benefits in Different Plans as Replacement and Reservation Rates (Moderate Mobility, Cliff-5 Vesting Rule)

Entry Age	Tenure	Money Pur.		Career Ave.		Final Average					
						10 Years		5 Years		3 Years	
		Rep.	Res.	Rep.	Res.	Rep.	Res.	Rep.	Res.	Rep.	Res.
20	0	1.24	0.90	2.01	1.46	4.33	3.14	5.09	3.70	5.44	3.96
	10	3.65	1.00	6.46	1.77	14.14	3.87	16.63	4.55	17.79	4.87
	20	4.50	1.00	9.02	2.00	20.25	4.49	23.80	5.28	25.47	5.65
	30	5.03	1.00	11.34	2.25	26.18	5.20	30.78	6.12	32.93	6.54
	40	5.32	1.00	13.18	2.48	31.25	5.87	36.73	6.90	39.31	7.38
30	0	1.06	0.89	2.52	2.11	4.46	3.75	5.25	4.40	5.62	4.71
	10	3.09	1.00	7.97	2.58	14.44	4.67	16.97	5.49	18.16	5.88
	20	3.72	1.00	10.72	2.88	20.08	5.39	23.60	6.34	25.25	6.78
	30	4.02	1.00	12.58	3.13	24.25	6.03	28.51	7.09	30.51	7.59
40	0	0.85	0.87	2.98	3.05	4.24	4.34	4.98	5.11	5.33	5.46
	10	2.42	1.00	9.10	3.76	13.34	5.51	15.69	6.48	16.79	6.94
	20	2.78	1.00	11.36	4.09	17.25	6.20	20.28	7.29	21.70	7.80
50	0	0.59	0.83	3.10	4.35	3.46	4.86	4.07	5.71	4.36	6.11
	10	1.59	1.00	8.76	5.50	10.08	6.33	11.85	7.44	12.68	7.96
60	0	0.24	0.68	1.87	5.33	1.87	5.33	1.87	5.33	2.00	5.70

percent benefit level), and the economic assumptions made at the outset, the accrued benefit as a percentage of the wage at retirement (as replacement rate) is 3.68. This is equivalent to a reservation rate of 1.53 in that the invested value at retirement of 1.53 percent of the wages received in this employment would buy the same annuity. Thus, aside from risk considerations (that may be important) the individual should be indifferent, in the mean, as between a career average pension plan coverage with one percent benefit level and a 1.53 percent wage increase received at age 30. Since the length of service in question is pensionable under the vesting

TABLE 2.11. Expected Virtual Benefits in Different Plans as Replacement and Reservation Rates (Moderate Mobility, Cliff-5 Vesting Rule)

Entry Age	Tenure	Money Pur. Rep.	Money Pur. Res.	Career Ave. Rep.	Career Ave. Res.	Final Average 10 Years Rep.	Final Average 10 Years Res.	Final Average 5 Years Rep.	Final Average 5 Years Res.	Final Average 3 Years Rep.	Final Average 3 Years Res.
20	0	3.42	0.86	10.00	2.51	15.28	3.83	17.97	4.51	19.23	4.82
	10	1.71	0.83	6.71	3.24	8.78	4.23	10.32	4.98	11.04	5.32
	20	0.86	0.78	4.27	3.87	4.88	4.41	5.73	5.19	6.13	5.55
	30	0.31	0.67	1.95	4.20	1.95	4.20	2.27	4.89	2.43	5.24
30	0	2.41	0.84	8.81	3.07	12.01	4.19	14.12	4.92	15.10	5.27
	10	0.98	0.78	4.78	3.84	5.51	4.43	6.48	5.21	6.93	5.57
	20	0.33	0.67	2.04	4.21	2.04	4.21	2.38	4.92	2.55	5.26
40	0	1.48	0.80	6.97	3.78	8.25	4.47	9.70	5.26	10.38	5.62
	10	0.39	0.68	2.43	4.26	2.43	4.26	2.84	5.00	3.04	5.35
50	0	0.67	0.71	4.09	4.38	4.12	4.41	4.84	5.18	5.18	5.54

rule being used (5 years of service) another way of interpreting the reservation rate of 1.53 would be that the career average plan in question is equivalent, in the mean, to a money purchase plan of 1.53 percent contribution level, in terms of the accrued benefit of cohort (30,20).

We see the impact of inflation (assumed to be 5 percent) in determining the value of accrued benefits very clearly in Table 2.9. For example, the replacement rate of 3.68 for cohort (30,20) in career average plans that can be bought by 1.53 percent of the wages received, reduces to 1.81 for cohort (20,20), corresponding only to 0.71 percent of wages. The results are 7.49 and 3.28 percent, respectively, for cohort (40,20). All these benefits relate to the same tenure of 20 years. They should have been comparable under a more age-neutral arrangement, as they are under the money purchase plan.

The effect of the earnings base used in defined benefit plans is also seen to be substantial, especially in relation to longer tenures. For example, the replacement rate of cohort (30,30) is seen to increase from 8.70 in career average plans to 18.94 in final 3 years' average plans. Note that a large part of the increase is due to leaving the career average mode, rather than the length of the averaging period as it varies from 3 to 10 years. However, this result is also highly dependent on tenure. The difference in replacement rates between career average and final 3 years' average plans declines significantly as tenure is reduced.

According to recent surveys, the participant-weighted mean benefit level in defined benefit plans is 1.10 percent with a range of 0.60–2.00 percent.[21] On this basis, our estimate for the replacement rate of a worker retiring with 35 years of service—cohort (30,35), not included in the tables—is 12.91 × 1.10 = 14.20 in career average plans and 29.46 × 1.10 = 32.41 in final 5 years' average plans. These compare with respective empirical findings of 13.56 and 32.83, recently reported as average replacement rates for workers retiring in 1977 with 35 years of service.[22]

Although traditionally well established, measurement of pension benefits at retirement through accrued benefit in the current job alone is not very useful for many purposes, for mobility is ignored. According to our moderate mobility scenario, for example, only about one in eight individuals who enter a job at the age of 30 will remain in this job until retirement at age 65 (Table 2.2). With respect to current employment, a more useful measure is the expected termination benefit. By definition, this is the weighted average of all possible termination benefits in an employment, according to probabilities with which such benefits (possible lengths of tenure) may arise. These are presented in Table 2.10.

As an example, consider again the age cohort 30 under the career average plan. We see that at the time of entry into a job covered by such a plan, a 30-year old individual may expect a replacement rate at retirement of 2.52. This benefit is equivalent to the invested value at retirement of 2.11 percent of the wages to be earned from that job until its termination. After 10 years on the job—i.e., cohort (40,10)—the expected replacement rate increases to 9.10 and the corresponding reservation rate is 3.76. Of this amount, 2.47 has already accrued on the basis of 10 pensionable years (Table 2.9). The balance of 6.63 represents the expected residual benefit associated with additional tenure in the job. Other entries in Table 2.9 for defined benefit plans are interpreted similarly. In the case of money purchase plans, it should be noted that the reservation rate is the same as the one percent contribution rate with respect to pensionable lengths of service (5 or more years of tenure). When a length of service is not yet pensionable, however, as in the case of cohorts with zero tenure, the reservation rate is less than the contribution rate. Clearly, the difference (one minus the reservation rate) is a measure of the risk of an unvested termination. Thus an individual entering a job at the age of 40 would be indifferent as between a noncontributory money purchase plan of one percent contribution rate and a wage increase of 0.87 percent.

Impacts of the period of accumulation and plan types on expected termination benefits can also be observed in Table 2.10. We see, for example, that expected termination benefit for entry age 40 under a final 3 years' average plan is nearly twice that under a career average plan. We also see that for a given entry age, the expected residual benefit from current employment (i.e., expected termination benefit minus accrued benefit) first increases and then decreases with tenure. For entry age 35, for example, the expected residual benefit in a career average plan, expressed as a replacement rate, increases from 2.77 at entry to 6.90 after 10 years on the job, to 6.96 after 15 years on the job. (Entries are not shown in the tables.) It then decreases until retirement. At retirement (tenure 30 for entry age 35) the accrued and termination benefits are equal. This would mean that a potential termination implies the largest benefit forfeiture, on the average, when preceded by about 15 years of service. This "critical" tenure is different for different age cohorts and plan types. It can be seen, however, that it is larger for younger ages of entry and in final earnings plans. Thus, in terms of mobility and efficient allocation of labor, pension expectations would be more restrictive under final earnings plans and, following vesting, in employments that start in younger years. (We shall return to this issue in Section 2.3.6 below.)

Just as accrued benefit is not a good proxy for termination benefit related to the current employment, the latter is not a good approximation for all future benefits of a given age-tenure cohort, for there could be several pensionable employments beyond the current employment. We introduced above the concept of virtual benefit to describe the cumulative pension benefit related to all the employments following the termination of the current employment. Expected virtual benefits are presented in Table 2.11 for selected cohorts. These are computed under the assumption that all the employments during the period of accrual of the virtual benefit are subject to the same vesting rule and plan characteristics. These may be different, however, from those governing the current employment. For example, the replacement rate of 8.81 as expected virtual benefit of cohort (30,0) under the career average plan does not specify the pension coverage of the current employment (which is just entered) as being career average. It refers only to the expected cumulative pension in career average plans from termination of the current employment to retirement. Note also that the virtual benefit would be zero if the current employment extends to retirement, or terminates closer to retirement than the eligibility requirements would allow.

The concept of virtual benefit is being proposed as a means of measuring the expectations of the worker from the private pension system as a whole, beyond the current employment. Termination benefit from the current employment plus virtual benefit beyond this employment constitutes a complete characterization of work life pension benefits.

Consider again the age cohort 30 and assume for the moment that all employments are covered by career average plans. At entry into a new job, the expected termination benefit from that job is 2.52 as replacement rate or 2.11 as reservation rate (Table 2.10). The expected benefit from all subsequent jobs, the virtual benefit, is 8.81 or 3.07. After five years on the job (entries not shown) the pension promise as replacement rate of the current employment is already larger than the pension promise of the subsequent jobs (6.21 against 5.49). Because of the shorter period of investment, however, the latter is higher as reservation rate (3.81 against 2.88). Thus while expected termination benefits increase with tenure, expected virtual benefits as replacement rates decrease. For the age cohort in question, the virtual benefit is negligible after 25 years on the current job and zero after 30 or more years.

In terms of virtual benefits, the main difference between career average and final average plans is that the expected virtual benefit decreases more rapidly with tenure in the current employment, the shorter the averaging period. Note again that as tenure in the current employment increases, the period of accumulation of virtual benefits decreases. Therefore, the observed difference is due to the fact that benefit accrual under final average plans becomes more sensitive to the length of the period of accrual, as we increase the wage base in computing benefits by decreasing the averaging period. This faster decrease in expected virtual benefits, coupled with the faster increase with tenure in expected termination benefits, can again be viewed as a stronger disincentive to mobility in final average plans.

2.3.3 Mobility and Benefits

It is clear from Table 2.9 that there is a strong negative correlation between frequent job changes and pension accumulation, even though all employment spells may be pensionable. For example, consider an individual who begins his or her work life at age 20 and plans to retire at age 60. Suppose that he or she is continuously employed in jobs that are all covered by final 5 years' average plans. If he or she works five years each for eight different employers, the total replacement rate at retirement will be only 9.30 (entries are not shown in Table 2.9). If 10 years are spent with each of four employers, then the total accrued benefit as replacement rate will be 10.92, corresponding to accrued benefits for cohorts (20,10), (30,10), (40,10) and (50,10). If the work life is made up of two employments of 20 years each, the employee will be entitled to a replacement rate of 14.65. Finally, if the person stays 40 years with the same employer, he or she will realize a replacement rate of 23.60. Note that each of the four sample career paths are made up of pensionable employments only. The observed increases in benefit, which are substantial, are due to increasing employment durations. Clearly, there is a very large number of possible career paths that can be constructed and evaluated through Table 2.9. If we take the weighted average benefit for *all* possible career paths, we arrive at the concept of expected work life benefits given in Tables 2.10 and 2.11. The weights are the probabilities (in this case under our moderate mobility scenario) with which those different paths would be realized.

In this context, consider a typical individual of moderate mobility over a work life of 45 years, from age 20 to age 65. Under very favorable circumstances, assume that this individual will be continuously employed in jobs that are all covered by 5-year final average plans with a one percent benefit level. According to Tables 2.10 and 2.11, the expected work life pension benefit, expressed as replacement rate at retirement, is 5.09 + 17.97 = 23.06. How could this result be assessed in view of a reasonable income goal? How sensitive is it to the mobility assumption?

In response to the second question, we repeated some of the calculations using our low and high mobility assumptions. The results are presented in Table 2.12 for expected termination and virtual benefits under money purchase, career average, and final 5 years' average plans. Evidently, accrued benefit is independent of the mobility assumption and Table 2.9 is still valid. Note also that Table 2.12 is computed only for entry ages where the beginning of the predictive period coincides with the start of the current employment. Results are again given both in terms of replacement rates at retirement (top figures) and reservation rates over the period of employment implied (bottom figures). Sum of the expected termination and virtual benefits for a given cohort is again the expected work life benefit.

In terms of our example above, involving cohort 20 and final 5 years' average plans, we see that the expected work life benefit is 13.73 + 16.02 = 29.75 percent of the wage at retirement under the low mobility scenario. The corresponding result under the high mobility assumption is 1.94 + 15.59 = 17.53. In spite of a rather liberal vesting rule (full vesting after 5 years of service) these results show the very substantial impact of mobility on expected pension benefits. Thus the distributions of work life pension benefits (from age 20 to age 65) for groups of high, moderate and low mobility workers will be centered around the respective mean replacement rates of 17.53, 23.06 and 29.75. These levels could be considered in-

TABLE 2.12. Expected Termination (TB) and Virtual Benefits (VB) under Low and High Mobility Assumptions° (Cliff-5 Vesting Rule)

| | Low Mobility | | | | | | High Mobility | | | | | |
| | Money Pur. | | Career Ave. | | 5 Years | | Money Pur. | | Career Ave. | | 5 Years | |
Entry Age	TB	VB	TB	VB	TB	VB	TB	VB	TB	VB	TB	VB
20	2.50	2.62	5.12	7.94	13.73	16.02	0.65	3.38	0.83	9.62	1.94	15.59
	0.97	0.95	1.98	2.86	5.31	5.77	0.80	0.74	1.02	2.12	2.39	3.42
30	2.03	1.82	5.60	6.80	12.27	11.88	0.58	2.39	1.18	8.60	2.31	12.79
	0.96	0.93	2.65	3.50	5.81	6.10	0.79	0.72	1.61	2.59	3.15	3.85
40	1.52	1.11	5.81	5.27	10.01	7.75	0.49	1.48	1.57	6.89	2.52	9.16
	0.95	0.91	3.62	4.33	6.29	6.37	0.77	0.68	2.47	3.15	3.97	4.19
50	0.98	0.50	5.30	3.07	7.11	3.72	0.36	0.66	1.84	4.06	2.37	4.72
	0.93	0.84	5.01	5.21	6.72	6.30	0.72	0.58	3.65	3.55	4.69	4.13

°Top entries are in replacement rates, bottom entries are in reservation rates. All are computed under a 5-year service requirement for vesting.

adequate in view of the generally accepted retirement income goals.

A frequent assumption regarding total retirement income goal, including social security benefits, is about half salary after a career of 30 to 35 years. Sometimes this goal is stated in graduated terms, depending on the level of final pay. Such guidelines are frequently based, however, on highly idealized scenarios in which there is full pension coverage and no job mobility (i.e., a single employer). Perhaps a more useful approach is to compare disposable incomes before and after retirement. It is generally held that at low-to-moderate income levels, a preretirement income equivalency would be attained by a postretirement income of about 75 percent of the preretirement total. The social security primary benefit can account for about 40 percent of the final earnings in these income groups, leaving 35 percent to private pension benefits and other retirement income sources. In order to approximate such a replacement rate under our moderate mobility assumption, we must further assume an average benefit level of over 1.50 percent. (The expected work life benefit of 23.06 is based on a uniform, one-percent benefit level.) This makes our already exceptional scenario—of continuous employment, full coverage, final 5 years' average plans, a work life of 45 years—totally unrealistic. Even under the low mobility assumption, the mean benefit amount of 29.75 falls short of expectations. In an industry with a 60 percent coverage rate, for example, this number should be adjusted down to a replacement rate of about 18. Clearly, these are just averages and some employees will receive more. But some will receive even less.

An examination of Table 2.12 reveals additional interesting points regarding the impact of mobility. Note, for example, that this impact is borne largely by expected termination benefits; expected virtual benefits are less sensitive to mobility. The latter is in part related to the fact that expected virtual benefits under low mobility are almost always lower than those under high mobility. Since virtual benefits accrue following the termination of current employment, lower mobility implies a longer duration for the current employment and therefore a shorter period of accrual for virtual benefits.

On general grounds, higher rates of employment mobility would have two interrelated effects on vested benefits: (1) reducing the length of a pensionable service and (2) dividing a long period of pensionable service in one employment into shorter periods of such service in several employments. The former effect is operational on all plans, but the latter is relevant only in final earnings plans where benefits vested for a given year of service are determined by wages earned in later years in the same employment. Thus, final earnings plans are doubly affected by mobility. This is reflected in the above findings by the fact that in terms of expected work life benefits (termination plus virtual) final average plans are more sensitive to mobility than career average or money purchase plans.

2.3.4 Vesting Rules and Benefits

Vesting signifies the right of the employee, on termination of employment, to a deferred life annuity based on pensionable service to the time of termination, paid for by the employer's contributions and any required employee's contribution. In concept, vesting is a reflection of the *pension promise* which evolved from a means of gratuity at the turn of the 20th century to the present prefunded, regulated, and rather complicated system. The historical form of the pension promise, "if you stay in my employ until retirement, I will pay you a pension of X dollars during your postretirement years," was in accord with the view of pensions as long-service rewards. This promise did not include any obligation on the part of the employer to fund the pension before the employee's retirement, any benefits related to the death of the employee or the termination of his or her employment before retirement, any commitment to continue employing the individual until retirement, or any guarantee that the promise would be made good if the employer went out of business.

By the 1930s some employers had extended the pension promise so that if an employee remained with the employer a predetermined number of years, the employer would assume a liability to pay a pension on retirement, whether the employee continued to work for the employer until retirement or not. The promise was not always that generous, however, involving a service requirement of 20 years or more. Conditions were also usually attached by which an employee could be denied pension if he or she were discharged for cause or ever acted later in some way considered disloyal to the former employer. In contributory plans, vesting nearly always was denied if the terminating employee chose to withdraw his or her contributions in cash.

As we noted in Section 1.2, the historical view of a pension plan as a "chain that fastens a person to his employer," resulting in a misallocation of human resources, has much to do with stringent vesting provisions. This view was changed first in Canada by the Ontario Pension Benefits Act of 1965 and then in the United States by the Employee Retirement Income Security Act (ERISA) of 1974. These legislations effectively replaced the concept of the "reward for long service" by that of a "benefit earned during working years," thus leading to the modern view of employment pensions as deferred wages. Since the introduction of these legislations, vesting rules have been further liberalized in both countries. The 10-year service requirement and its alternatives in the U.S. have been effectively reduced to 5 years for tax qualification by the 1986 tax legislation. Some Canadian provinces, as well as the Canadian federal government went further and recently legislated 2-year vesting rules and portable plans.

In spite of these recent developments, vesting, next to portability, remains as one of the least understood features of a pension system. In this section, we take a closer look at the comparative effects of vesting rules on pension benefits in different plans.

We expect that the vesting rule should have a marginal effect on expected benefits and that nothing much should be lost due to vesting requirements in the low termination sector. As mobility increases, however, the vesting rule becomes a critical factor, especially in career average and money purchase plans. On the other hand, we expect that the final earnings plans should be relatively insensitive to vesting requirements, due to the fact that pension benefits related to different ages depend more heavily in these plans on the age at termination.

These expectations are well reflected in Table 2.13 which presents the expected termination and virtual benefits under the 2-year and 10-year service requirements for full vesting. For example, expected work life benefit for entry age 30 increases 30 percent in career average plans and

TABLE 2.13. Expected Termination (TB) and Virtual Benefits (VB) under Cliff-2 and Cliff-10 Vesting Rules°

| | Cliff-2 | | | | | | Cliff-10 | | | | | |
| | Money Pur. | | Career Ave. | | 5 Years | | Money Pur. | | Career Ave. | | 5 Years | |
Entry Age	TB	VB	TB	VB	TB	VB	TB	VB	TB	VB	TB	VB
20	1.34	3.83	2.04	11.06	5.12	18.98	1.10	2.87	1.96	8.44	5.03	16.28
	0.97	0.96	1.49	2.77	3.72	4.76	0.80	0.72	1.42	2.12	3.65	4.08
30	1.16	2.74	2.59	9.89	5.32	15.15	0.93	1.95	2.41	7.19	5.13	12.37
	0.97	0.96	2.17	3.45	4.46	5.28	0.78	0.68	2.02	2.51	4.30	4.31
40	0.94	1.75	3.12	8.10	5.12	10.78	0.73	1.12	2.75	5.24	4.74	7.84
	0.96	0.95	3.20	4.39	5.25	5.84	0.75	0.61	2.82	2.84	4.86	4.24
50	0.68	0.86	3.40	5.29	4.36	5.98	0.48	0.36	2.65	2.14	3.58	2.73
	0.95	0.92	4.77	5.66	6.11	6.40	0.67	0.38	3.71	2.29	5.02	2.92

°Top entries are in replacement rates, bottom entries are in reservation rates. All are computed under the moderate mobility scenario.

35.4 percent in money purchase plans, from the 10-year to the 2-year rule. The same increase is only 17 percent in final 5 years' plans. Another important observation is that while the impact of the vesting rule is marginal on the termination benefits of younger cohorts in defined benefit plans, in the money purchase plan substantial changes are indicated for all cohorts. For example, again in passing from the 10-year to the 2-year rule, the expected termination benefit of entry age 20 increases 4 percent in career average plans, only 1.8 percent in final 5 years' plans, but almost 22 percent in money purchase plans. (We will have more about the impact of the vesting rule in relation to the distribution of pension benefits and costs in Chapter 3.)

2.3.5 Coverage and Portability

Lack of universal private pension coverage and limited portability have been the center of much public debate both in the United States and

Canada. These issues have been paid a great deal of attention by almost every pension commission or pension study group. We have reviewed the important historical developments and summarized the recent statistics regarding coverage and portability in Chapter 1. In preparation for some of the results to be developed and discussed below, earlier in this chapter we also studied the impacts of coverage and portability on the work life pensionable service. We now look at these influences on work life pension benefits.

The most frequently used definition of pension coverage involves current participation in a pension or profit sharing plan. According to this definition, and as we noted in Chapter 1, approximately 50 percent of the total private wage and salary employees in North America are currently covered by a pension plan. Some suggest that it is more appropriate to define pension coverage with respect to employees who currently meet plan participation standards. ERISA does not require private sector pension plans to cover workers who are under age 25, who work less than 1,000 hours a year, and who have less than one year of service with their companies. These standards are preserved under the 1986 Tax Reform Act in defining qualified plans. For workers meeting these criteria, the coverage rate is over 60 percent.[23] It should be noted, however, that less than 60 percent of the public and private work force meets the criteria in question.

Another way to analyze coverage is to consider *covered jobs* rather than *covered people*. This consideration is more convenient for our purposes in view of our characterization of employment dynamics by a two-state process through covered and noncovered employments.

As we argued before, coverage alone is not a useful measure of the effectiveness of a pension system. The amount of retirement income that the private pension plan participants are likely to receive depends also on a number of other factors. Important among these factors is the portability of pension rights. Social Security in the United States and the Canada Pension Plan in Canada provide complete portability for their benefits. The employee with ten different jobs and the employee with only one, each contributing on the same level of earnings for the same period to age 65, may expect to receive the same amount of pension. The design characteristics that make this perfect portability possible include the coverage of all employees in the same plan so that they are all subject to the same benefit formula, funding method, contributions, retirement age, and other provisions; immediate vesting of benefits; and the prohibition of the transfer of funds to any other pension vehicle. On the other hand, employment pension plans exhibit a large variety. This lack of homogeneity makes universal portability among private pension plans virtually impossible.

Earlier or immediate vesting has often been proposed as an alternative to portability. Even if immediate vesting were legislated for all private pension plans, however, the result would not be the same as a transferable pension that could be carried from one employment to the next throughout a work life. Although a fixed amount of pension would be left behind with each employer, the value of these will erode with inflation in the absence of any indexation. When the previously vested benefits are based on final earnings, final earnings at retirement could be much larger than final earnings at earlier terminations, especially during younger years. Even with only one change of job in a defined benefit pension system, an employee may suffer a significant loss from this break in service without portability.

There is another limitation from the employee's point of view in substituting earlier or immediate vesting for portability. This is the fact that, in most contributory defined benefit plans, cost of the benefit vested in younger employees may be smaller than the value of their own contributions. For if "locked-in" at the time of termination, an employee's own contributions may buy all or more of the vested annuity. Yet the individual has no opportunity to improve the eventual pension by investing the money in other ways. Earlier vesting could, therefore, be seen as a further restriction on the freedom of younger employees. At the root of the difficulty in trying to solve the portability problem with earlier vesting is the fact that the vesting rule, by its nature, operates when service accrual stops. Even if an employee is immediately eligible to join the pension plan of the next employer, the new plan would involve only service from that time forward.

There have been two partially successful approaches to the provision of portability, as distinct from the use of a more liberal vesting provision: reciprocal transfer agreements and intrasystem portability under multi-employer pension plans. Reciprocal arrangements within families of pension plans—such as those among some public sector plans, employer associations, and unions—have been an effective means of preserving pension rights on change of employment within the system. One example is the Canadian Federal Public Service Superannuation Administration under which the new employer assumes the liability for the total pension of the employee including the service rendered to the previous employer.[24] The "exporting" employer, together with the employee are responsible for the contributions to be made to the "importing" employer for services rendered to the former. This type of reciprocal arrangement imposes relatively greater burdens on the next employer for obvious reasons. Other arrangements have also been developed in practice that shift more of this burden to the previous employer, according to some pro rata formula that takes into account the salary increase with the next employer.[25]

In any case, as we pointed out in Chapter 1, in order to be workable in practice, reciprocity requires homogeneity of employers, plan types and employee occupational groups among participating organizations. Mobility patterns between different pairs of plans must also be in balance to avoid financial bias. For these reasons, reciprocal arrangements that achieve full portability have seen limited success among government plans, municipalities and educational institutions. There has been little interest in the idea among private sector employers. Traditionally, employers in the private sector have been reluctant to make it easier for their long-services more-experienced employees to move to a competing firm. The fact is that portability, in general, and reciprocal transfer arrangements, in particular, facilitate employee mobility. Longer service employees who might be reluctant to move because of an interest in pension benefits would be more willing to change jobs given full portability. In the context of reciprocal arrangements, the situation is made more difficult because of the prerequisite similarities of the organizations involved. Thus such an arrangement requires the cooperation of similar firms but in the private sector similar firms compete more than they cooperate.

Intrasystem portability through multi-employer pension plans is achieved by utilizing the homogeneity of a group of employers to establish a common plan, usually based on a collective agreement. The arrangement provides portability of pension rights, accompanied by a transfer of the underlying assets, for members of participating plans. This transfer of assets separates multi-employer plans from reciprocal arrangements. In addition, an employee's membership in multi-employer plans is typically through a particular union rather than through a given employer. Through these arrangements, it has been possible to extend pension coverage to highly mobile workers in certain trades; they have been rather popular, for example, in the construction industry.

In addition to unionization and high rates of mobility, multi-employer plans have been popular in industries characterized by a relatively large number of small firms. Use of large amounts of skilled labor, intense competition, and occupational attachment rather than firm attachment of the work force are some other characteristics that have been associated with the multi-employer pattern. On the supply side, by joining in a larger pension fund, the participating small employers have been able to make use of economies of scale in management.[26]

Reciprocal transfer agreements and multi-employer plans provide portability for the particular groups they apply; however, intersystem portability, portability between these arrangements and single employer plans, and portability among the latter are generally lacking. And, as we noted before, immediate vesting is not a satisfactory approximation to portability because it still places a heavy penalty on broken service. Indeed, universal portability is probably not achievable and should not be expected from a private pension system. This implies varying degrees of portability related to different industries and to employments that an individual in these industries is likely to encounter in his or her work life. What is the impact of a given rate of portability on the accumulation of work life pension benefits? How does portability interact with mobility, pension coverage, vesting rules and plan types? We now turn to an examination of these issues. For this purpose, we use an extension of the model we introduced in Section 2.2.2 for pensionable service, by restricting our attention to work life benefits.

At issue is the expected pension benefit during a work life which starts at age t with an employment of given pension status (covered or not covered) and terminates at age T with retirement. First, consider the contribution of the first employment. Clearly, there is no contribution if this employment is not covered. If it is covered, then consider the length of time spent in a sequence of one or more covered and portable employments. This sequence would eventually terminate either with retirement or with a transition to a noncovered or covered but not portable employment. In the first case, $B(T-t,T-t)$ will accrue. In the second case, suppose it terminates before retirement with length $u \geqslant s$. Then $B(T-t,u)$ will accrue. As before, the function $B(T-t,x)$ represents the accrued benefit resulting from an employment of length x that started $T-t$ time units before retirement.

Similarly, we can formalize the contribution of all subsequent employments. In order for such a contribution to exist, there must be an entry into a covered state sometime before retirement, with sufficient time left to vest the pension. Say that such an entry takes place at time $T-t-u$, meaning u time units before retirement where $s \leqslant u \leqslant T-t$. Given such an entry, either the ensuing sequence of covered and portable employments lasts until retirement, resulting in $B(u,u)$, or, this sequence has a lesser duration $x < u$, resulting in $B(u,x)$. Probabilities of all the underlying events can be constructed from mobility data and mathematical formulae can be developed for computations.[27]

In Figure 2.4, Figure 2.5 and Figure 2.6, we present some numerical examples for expected work life benefits in career average plans, last three years' average plans, and money purchase plans. Both defined benefit plans are again based on a one percent benefit level, but the contribution rate in the money purchase plan is now 6 percent. In all cases, the work life extends from age 20 to age 65 and the first employment is assumed not covered by a pension plan. The length of stay distributions in covered and noncovered employments were represented on the basis of moderate and high mobility data, respectively.

The results are given as they correlate with the vesting rule (s=2,5,10), coverage rate (p=0.25, 0.50, 0.75) and portability (0.1 to 1.0). As in Section 2.2.2, we assumed in these computations that the probability c of moving into a covered employment, following a termination, does not depend on the pension status of the terminated job. This probability was related to the coverage rate p and mean lengths of stay in covered and noncovered employments. This representation is an approximation based on a stationary

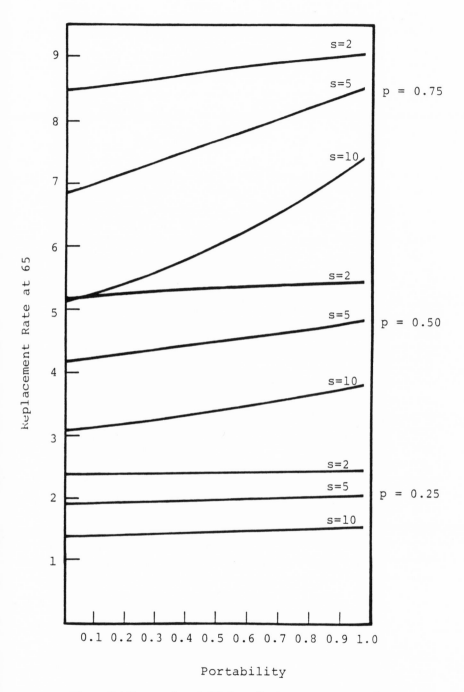

Figure 2.4 Expected work life benefits in career average plans.

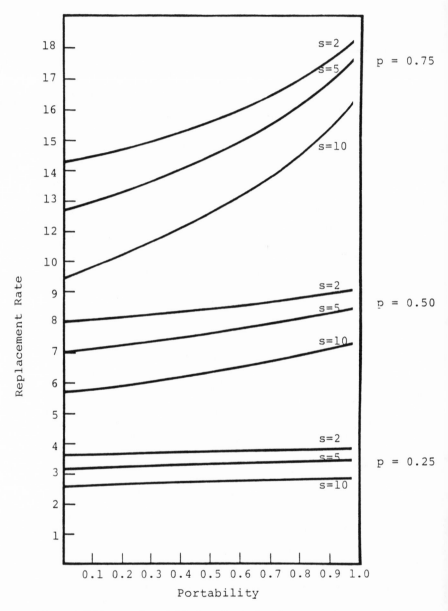

Figure 2.5 Expected work life benefits in last three years' average plans.

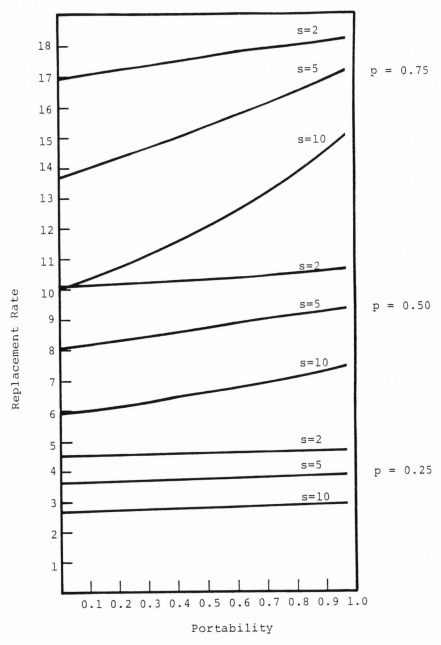

Figure 2.6 Expected work life benefits in money purchase plans.

73

employment termination process. (The relationship between c and p is depicted in the insert of Figure 2.1.)

It can be seen from the figures that the impact of coverage rate is substantial in all plans. It is also clear that the expected benefit is not a linear function of the coverage rate. That is, other things being the same, increase in benefit from p=0.50 to p=0.75, for example, is larger than the increase in benefit from p=0.25 to p=0.50. This nonlinearity is more pronounced under more stringent vesting rules and under the final average plans.

Portability is more effective under higher rates of coverage and more stringent vesting requirements. When the rate of coverage is as low as 0.25, the extent of portability appears irrelevant. On the other hand, with a coverage rate of 0.75, the expected benefit increases under the 10-year vesting rule from about 9.4 if there is no portability to about 15.6 if portability is almost universal.[28] This effect is mitigated by a less stringent vesting rule and a defined benefit formula that is less sensitive to wage growth. Thus the increases in benefit with increasing portability are relatively less pronounced in career average plans. Another observation that can be made relates to the combined impact of plan type, vesting rule and portability. While a very liberal vesting rule (i.e., s=2) appears to be an effective substitute for portability in career average and money purchase plans, such is not the case in final average plans.

2.3.6 Pensions as Disincentives to Mobility

In terms of mobility and pension accrual, the previous discussion has generally moved from mobility to pension accrual. Thus a highly mobile individual is not very likely to vest his or her pension, especially in the presence of stringent vesting requirements. Even after vesting, benefits will erode with inflation from employment termination to retirement. Consequently, mobility has an adverse effect on pension accrual.

This relationship could also be examined in the reverse direction. We may regard the expected pension as the independent variable, as it were, and be concerned with the extent to which this will inhibit mobility. From what we have seen so far, it is clear that by terminating an employment covered by a pension plan, a worker may suffer a substantial loss in remaining lifetime compensation. The main reason for this occurrence is the same as before—that the current job benefits would improve with wage growth reflecting inflation, but past benefits would not. As we noted in Chapter 1, it can be argued that this phenomenon—of pension-induced immobility— may have been responsible in part for the currently observable low levels of job mobility in some of the declining industries.

In this section, we develop a framework for the measurement of disincentives to mobility induced by pension expectations. The procedure is based on comparing the expected pension benefit from the current employment with accrued benefit from this employment plus expected benefit from a potential new employment.

As an example, consider first an individual who has 20 years on a job that he or she had entered at the age of 20. Assume that this employment is covered by a 3-year final average plan with one-percent benefit level. From Table 2.9, the accrued benefit as replacement rate is 3.05 and from Table 2.10, the expected termination benefit is 25.47. Now, consider a potential job change to an employment covered again by a career average plan of one-percent benefit level. The new job would have been entered at the age of 40, and, according to Table 2.10, it would have had an expected termination benefit of 2.98. Consequently, the tradeoff is between 25.47, as the expected termination benefit from the current employment, and $3.05 + 2.98 = 6.03$, as the already accrued benefit from the current employment plus the expected benefit from the potential new employment. The difference is 19.44 in favor of the current employment. Thus this potential job change would induce, other things being equal, a replacement rate loss of 19.44. Finally, again from Table 2.10, we see that with respect to employments that start at age 40, the loss in question corresponds to a reservation rate of $19.44 \times 3.05/2.98 = 19.90$. It would take a wage increase in the new job of nearly 20 percent for the individual to be indifferent between the two alternatives!

In general, for an individual of attained age t+y, tenure y, the accrued benefit as replacement rate from the current employment (CE) is $B_{CE}(T-t,y)$ and the expected termination benefit is $\bar{M}_{CE}(t,y)$. A potential new employment (PE) would start at age t+y with no tenure. It may have a different pension coverage, with a different vesting rule; it may not even be covered by a pension plan. The expected termination benefit from this potential employment is $\bar{M}_{PE}(t+y,0)$. Consequently, the expected loss or gain induced by a potential change in employment can be expressed as:

$$D(t,y) = \bar{M}_{CE}(t,y) - B_{CE}(T-t,y) - \bar{M}_{PE}(t+y,0).$$

Clearly, $\bar{M}_{PE} = 0$ if the potential job is not covered by a pension plan. This loss or gain is compensated by a wage increase or decrease in the new employment of $D(t,y)/\bar{M}°_{MP}(t+y,0)$ where the denominator represents the expected termination benefit as replacement rate under a money purchase plan of one-percent contribution level and full and immediate vesting, starting at age t+y.

Additional examples for entry age 30 computed from the above formulas are presented in Table 2.14. It should be noted that if the current employment is covered by a final average plan, then the expected pension loss increases rapidly with tenure in the current employment. On the other hand, losses related to moves out of career average plans appear marginal except

TABLE 2.14. Expected Losses in Replacement Rates (Rep.) and Reservation Wage Increases (Res.) Induced by Potential Job Changes

Tenure in Curr. Empl.[1]	Pension Coverage of Current/Next Employment									
	3 yr./3 yr.		3 yr./5 yr.		3 yr./10 yr.		3 yr./CA		3 yr./NC	
	Rep.	Res.	Rep.	Res.	Rep.	Res.	Rep.	Res.	Rep.	Res.
10	11.31	11.58	11.66	11.93	12.40	12.69	13.66	13.98	16.64	17.03
20	14.68	20.60	14.97	21.00	15.58	21.86	15.94	22.37	19.04	26.72

	10 yr./3 yr.		10 yr./5 yr.		10 yr./10 yr.		10 yr./CA		10 yr./NC	
	Rep.	Res.	Rep.	Res.	Rep.	Res.	Rep.	Res.	Rep.	Res.
10	7.90	8.09	8.25	8.44	8.99	9.20	10.25	10.49	13.23	13.54
20	10.79	15.14	11.08	15.55	11.69	16.40	12.05	16.41	15.15	21.26

	CA/3 yr.		CA/5 yr.		CA/10 yr.		CA/CA		CA/NC	
	Rep.	Res.	Rep.	Res.	Rep.	Res.	Rep.	Res.	Rep.	Res.
10	1.43	1.46	1.78	1.82	2.52	2.58	3.78	3.87	6.76	6.92
20	2.68	3.76	2.97	4.17	3.58	5.02	3.94	5.53	7.04	9.88

[1]Entry age = 30.
NC = Not covered.
CA = Career Average.

when the next employment is not covered by a pension plan. With the same exception, it is also interesting to note that the pension coverage of the next employment is of secondary importance in moves following long job tenures. In such cases, most of the loss is due to the interruption of a long job tenure rather than to the change in plan type.

It should be emphasized that no decision problem is being implied or solved by this procedure regarding job changes. What we have is simply a framework, consistent with our aggregate model of mobility for the measurement of the penalty placed by pension coverage on potential moves out of an employment; however, this framework has one apparent shortcoming. So far, in comparing the two alternatives (of staying with the current job or moving to a new job) we ignored employment beyond these jobs. This would not have caused any conceptual difficulty, if the mean residual duration of the current employment of cohort (t,y) were the same as the mean duration of employment for cohort (t+y,0). As this is not in general true, we have compared above the two alternatives over intervals that are not probabilistically equivalent. One way to improve the procedure is to incorporate benefits that might accrue from termination of the current employment (or its alternatives) to retirement. This requires some assumptions regarding pension coverage during the period of accumulation of what we called virtual benefits.

A useful representation is to assume that upon termination of an employment, an individual enters into an employment covered by pension plan type j with probability, p_j, for $j=1,2,\ldots,m$, where m is the number of different plan types, and $p_1+p_2+\ldots+p_m\leqslant 1$. Probability of entering into a noncovered employment would then be $p_0=1-(p_1+p_2+\ldots+p_m)$. Now let $\tilde{M}_{AV}(t,y)$ denote the weighted average of the virtual benefits induced by different plans on cohort (t,y). Clearly, if the probabilities p_j, $j=0,1,\ldots,m$, are typical of the job opportunities that an individual is likely to encounter, or if the individual chooses his or her jobs at random and p_j's are respective proportions, then $\tilde{M}_{AV}(t,y)$ is the expected virtual benefit of cohort (t,y), the expectation being taken over all applicable types of pension coverage, including noncoverage, of all future employments.

Now, in addition to the current employment (CE) and a potential new employment (PE), the information $\tilde{M}_{AV}(t,y)$ is also available to cohort (t,y). As such, this last information reflects what can be expected from the pension system beyond the current employment or its immediate potential alternative. We now modify the computation of expected loss as:

$$D(t,y) = \tilde{M}_{CE}(t,y) + \tilde{M}_{AV}(t,y)$$
$$- [B_{CE}(T-t,y) + M_{PE}(t+y,0) + \tilde{M}_{AV}(t+y,0)].$$

The first line on the right-hand side of this formula represents the expected work life pension benefit if no change occurs at time t+y and the second line is the expected benefit following a potential change. By a potential change, we mean the termination of the current employment covered by a given pension plan, with accrued benefit B_{CE}, followed by potential entry into a new employment covered by a possible different (but again given) pension plan. We use the word "potential" to emphasize that time t+y is not necessarily the time at which an actual change of employment and pension plan takes place. But *if it were*, the expected loss in replacement rate at retirement would have been as above.

The reservation wage that corresponds to D(t,y) can be expressed as before by dividing it with the value of wages, from t+y to retirement, in the sense of a one-percent money purchase plan under full and immediate vesting. The result is the reservation wage rate, as a constant fraction of wage from t+y to retirement, that corresponds to the loss (or gain) in the expected replacement rate differential. Note that, as opposed to the earlier representation, the underlying time period may now include more than one employment.

As an example, consider again the potential move from an employment covered by a 3-year final average plan to an employment covered by a career-average plan of a 40 year old worker with 20 years on the job. Considering defined benefit plans only, assume that beyond the current employment, or its immediate potential replacement, the probability of a covered employment is 0.60 and of a noncovered employment is $p_0 = 0.40$. Given that an employment is covered, probability that it is covered by a career average plan is 0.28. Similarly, probabilities for 10-year, 5-year, and 3-year final average plans are 0.11, 0.54, and 0.07, respectively. These probabilities approximate the distribution of defined benefit plan types in practice. Consequently, upon termination of an employment, the probability of entering into an employment covered by a career average plan is $P_{CA} = 0.60 \times 0.28 = 0.168$. Similarly, we find $P_{F10} = 0.066$, $P_{F5} = 0.324$, and $P_{F3} = 0.042$.

For the cohort in question, we also have:

$\tilde{M}_{CE}(20,20) =$	25.47	(Table 2.10)
$B_{CE}(20,20) =$	3.05.	(Table 2.9)
$M_{PE}(40, 0) =$	2.98.	(Table 2.10)

$$\tilde{M}_{AV}(20,20) = \begin{aligned} &0.168 \times 4.27 + 0.066 \times 4.88 \\ &+ 0.324 \times 5.73 + 0.042 \times 6.13 \\ &= 3.15. \end{aligned}$$

(Table 2.11)

$$\tilde{M}_{AV}(40, 0) = \begin{aligned} &0.168 \times 6.97 + 0.066 \times 8.25 \\ &+ 0.324 \times 9.70 + 0.042 \times 10.38 \\ &= 5.29. \end{aligned}$$

(Table 2.11)

Using these results in the above formula, we find:

$$D(t,y) = 25.47 + 3.15 - (3.05 + 2.98 + 5.29) = 17.30$$

as the expected loss in replacement rate. This compares with the approximation 19.44 that we computed earlier by considering only the current and the potential new employments.

NOTES

1. This data set was made available to the author by the Royal Commission on the Status of Pensions in Ontario. It also provided the basis for the mobility assumptions used in studies by the author for the Commission. See, for example, Balcer and Sahin, 1984, and Yves Balcer and Izzet Sahin, "Modeling the Impact of Pension Reform—A Case Study," *The Journal of Risk and Insurance, 49* (1982), pp. 158-191.

2. The terms *mean* and *expected value* are used interchangeably throughout the book in the usual statistical sense. To be more exact, we should talk about the *expected value of a random variable* or, equivalently, *the mean of its distribution.*

3. *Completed employment* or *completed length of service* are used in contrast to *tenure* which is of a currently active and, therefore, incomplete employment.

4. For a derivation of this formula, see Balcer and Sahin, 1983, p. 188.

5. The terms *pensionable service, creditable service* and *qualifying service* are used interchangeably.

6. See H.E. Winklevoss, *Pension Mathematics with Numerical Illustrations,* Pension Research Council, Irwin, Homewood, Illinois, 1977, pp. 178-179.

7. "Cliff vesting" is a common term used to describe full vesting after a specified number of years of service. This is contrasted with "graded vesting" where the conversion of tenure to pensionable service is affected gradually over a number of years. In the sequel, we sometimes use the term "cliff-s" to abbreviate "full vesting" after s years of service, for a specific value of s.

8. For a proof, see Izzet Sahin and Yves Balcer, "Qualifying Service under ERISA Vesting Standards—A Comparative Analysis", *The Journal of Risk and Insurance,* (1979), pp. 492-495.

9. Ibid., p. 492, note 7.

10. Again, this requirement can be weakened and termination rates can be allowed to increase with tenure over certain intervals without changing the conclusion.

11. Kotlikoff and Smith, p. 191.

12. For mathematical forms, see Balcer and Sahin, 1984, pp. 681-686 and Sahin, 1986, pp. 18-43.

13. For mathematical aspects, see Sahin, 1978, and Balcer and Sahin, 1983.

14. See note 13 above.

15. Most of the data from recent surveys are collected, organized and annotated in Kotlikoff and Smith.

16. Ibid., pp. 237-244.

17. See Sahin, 1986, for general forms.

18. See note 17 above.

19. See note 17 above.

20. See Ippolito, pp. 103-105.

21. Kotlikoff and Smith, p. 210.

22. Ibid., note 16.

23. President's Commission on Pension Policy, p. 18.

24. *Report of the Royal Commission on the Status of Pensions in Ontario,* vol. 2, 1980, p. 31.

25. See note 24 above.

26. For more on multi-employer plans see, for example, M.E. McDonald, *Reciprocity among Private Multiemployer Pension Plans,* Pension Research Council, Irwin, Homewood, Illinois, 1975.

27. See Balcer and Sahin, 1983.

28. In interpreting these results, the reader should bear in mind the assumption that the first employment is not covered by a pension plan.

3
Plan Perspective

So far, we have taken the worker for a unit of analysis and concerned ourselves with the dynamics of pension accrual. Thus the worker is fixed, as it were, while the employers and pension plans are changing. In this context, the work life benefit function that we introduced in Section 2.3.1, for example, represents the ultimate benefit to be derived by a worker from a career membership in pension plans. In this representation the worker is identified with age (t) and tenure (y) in the current employment. If we take y = 0 and specialize t to an age that is representative of the beginning age for a typical work life (or for pension plan membership), then our benefit function would refer to the total length of a typical work life from its beginning to retirement. As an example, we see from Tables 2.10 and 2.11 that under 5 years' average plans with one-percent benefit level and cliff-5 vesting rule, the expected work life benefits is 5.09 + 17.97 = 23.06 as replacement rate at retirement for an individual who starts his or her work life at the age of 20 and expects to retire at 65.

From the *plan perspective*, there is another interpretation of this number. For this, we must first reconcile the work life perspective with the traditional approach of taking the firm or the plan as the unit of analysis. The firm-oriented approach to the measurement of pension benefits and costs, in addition to the usual economic assumptions, requires the distribution of age at entry and the distribution of age (or tenure) at termination, given an entry age. For a given firm, there is no need for these two distributions to be compatible. They have to be compatible, however, over all firms or for a representative firm in which case it becomes immaterial whether it is the job or the individual that is changing. Therefore, the num-

81

ber 23.06 in the above example can also be interpreted as a measure of the pension benefit due to an *employment position* covered by a pension plan. We will refer to this benefit as the *plan benefit*.

Like the benefit measures we discussed in Chapter 2, plan benefit is also unadjusted for mortality. In the present context, this is an omission as the concept of plan benefit is meaningful mainly as a measure of the obligation of a pension plan on behalf of a covered employment, and this potential obligation will be affected by mortality. We prefer, however, to introduce mortality in passing from plan benefits to pension costs. Thus plan benefit is viewed as a gross interim measure that, in a way, links pension benefits to pension costs.

Although the theoretical foundations are essentially the same as before, this chapter is based on a different methodology. The data base is also slightly revised. Examples are computed using discrete mathematics with a year as the time step. Thus, the "actual" rates of termination given in Table 2.1 are used to represent employee mobility, rather than fitting continuous probability distributions to these. Economic assumptions are also expanded and slightly modified to better serve the objectives of the chapter.

Following a review in Section 3.1 of the data and assumptions, expected values of pension benefits and pension costs are discussed in Section 3.2. This includes a look at the impact of inflation on plan benefits and costs in contributory and noncontributory plans. As in Chapter 2, expected benefits are measured as a fraction of the wage at retirement. Pension costs, on the other hand, are measured as a percentage of the payroll. Both are treated as random variables; their variances and distributions are discussed in Section 3.3. The effects of mobility, vesting rule, retirement age and plan type on the variability of benefits and costs are quantified in this section, not only in terms of summary measures but also by constructing the actual distributions. The chapter is concluded with two case studies adopted from recent applications of the methodology to real world situations. Section 3.4 features a "steady state" analysis of the pension cost differentials caused by some "reform" initiatives in a pension plan or a pension system. Section 3.5 then presents a "dynamic" analysis of how pension benefits and pension costs evolve in time as these initiatives take effect. The reform initiatives considered include the indexation of benefits of active employees and deferred benefits of terminated employees.

3.1 DATA AND ASSUMPTIONS

In this chapter, we consider three different plan designs: a career average plan (CA), a last 5 years' average plan (FA), and a money purchase plan (MP). We drop for brevity the other final earnings plans we included in Chapter 2. The benefit level in both defined benefit plans is taken as one percent. The contribution level in the money purchase plan is assumed to be 6 percent for approximate comparability with the other two plans. As before, results for other benefit or contribution levels will be proportional to the results reported below.

In most of the discussion, all three plans are considered both in their contributory and noncontributory modes. In the former mode, the employee contributions are taken as 2.5 percent in defined benefit plans and 3 percent in the MP plan. In contributory defined benefit plans, when an employee terminates before vesting or dies before or after vesting but prior to retirement, he or she is assumed to get the return of his or her own contributions. Interest at a specified rate is added to these reimbursements, if indicated by the policy configuration used. If, at the time of a vested exit from a contributory defined benefit plan, the accumulated contributions could buy more than the accrued pension, the plan benefit is adjusted upward correspondingly. In some applications discussed later in the chapter, the excess contributions are assumed returned to the employees, with interest at the fund rate. In some other applications, this assumption is supplemented by the provision that at least one-half of the deferred annuity in contributory defined benefit plans be paid for by employer contributions.

The earliest plan membership age is taken to be 25. Two alternative retirement ages are considered: 65 as the normal and 60 as the early retirement age. In all cases, plan benefits are computed as a fraction of the wage at the normal retirement age with actuarially reduced annuities for the early retirement age.

Mobility and vesting rule assumptions of Chapter 2 are retained. The moderate mobility assumption is represented by the termination rate schedule given in Table 2.1. High and low mobility assumptions correspond, respectively, to termination rates that are 50 percent higher and 50 percent lower than these. As before, we consider cliff vesting rules that require 10, 5 and 2 years of service.

Mortality rates used are based on recent Group Annuity Mortality (GAM) tables as related to the actual experience of pension plan members. This data implies life expectancies at ages 60 and 65 of 19.23 and 15.57 years, respectively.

In terms of economic assumptions, most of the calculations are carried out under the alternative inflation rate assumptions of 4 and 6 percent. This amounts to a 2 percent range around the 5 percent rate used in Chapter 2. The real rates of interest and wage growth were taken as 2.5 and 2 percent, respectively. The former is later extended to a range from 1 to 3 percent. Based on recent studies, the following wage profile was adopted:

Age	20	25	30	35	40–65
Wage Index	.40	.65	.85	.93	1.00

As in Chapter 2, the methodology used in this chapter also assumes that the impact of inflation is fully reflected in wages and that the real interest rate is unaffected by inflation. In reality, neither inflation nor the real rate of return would remain constant over time. Plan benefits in defined benefit plans, for example, would be independent of the probabilistic nature of the wage path, given that the expected wage remains unchanged in each period. This is no longer true for plan costs, however, even if the rates of interest and wage growth were perfectly correlated with inflation. What is required for a more accurate representation of reality is the incorporation in the methodolgy of a joint distribution of inflation, wage growth, and interest rate possibilities. While such a methodology would be workable on conceptual grounds, it would be far too complicated for our purposes here. For the same reason, the fund rate of return, which generally exhibits far greater variation than the inflation or the wage growth rate, is not modeled probabilistically. Instead, we chose a deterministic representation supported by sensitivity analysis.

3.2 EXPECTED BENEFITS AND COSTS

In passing from work life benefits to plan benefits and costs, we no longer need the assumption that all employments are covered by a pension plan and that all pension plans (in one's work life) are similar. We may also set aside the questions of partial coverage and portability, for we are now concerned with a given firm or plan. These assumptions are replaced by a "*representative*" firm (or plan) assumption, however, especially in terms of the age-tenure mix of the plan members.

These simplifications enable us to provide a more complete characterization of plan benefits and costs in terms of their variability and distribution. These additional measures are of interest not only for employers with regard to the variability and distribution of pension costs but also in terms of public policy issues related to the effectiveness and regulation of the pension system.

3.2.1 Expected Plan Benefits

Expected plan benefit is the average pension benefit, not adjusted for mortality, that would accrue relative to an employment position. It is measured as a fraction of the wage at retirement (i.e., the replacement rate). The period of accrual is from the age of first membership in the plan (assumed 25 in the examples of this section) to the age of retirement (60 or 65). As noted before, this benefit concept corresponds to the work life benefit concept of Chapter 2. In that case, under the assumptions of continuous employment, full coverage, and so on, the scenario was one of an individual who starts his or her work life at the age of 25 and moves in and out of different employments until the retirement age. From the plan perspective, we now assume that every terminating employee is replaced by a new one and, instead of following the individual, we follow the pension accrual process as it operates on the successive occupants of an employment position. Over a work-life-equivalent period (i.e., from 25 to 65), total pension in the plan would be similar, on the average, to work life pension if the age distribution of the leavers is similar to the age distribution of the entrants.[1] As noted before, these two distributions must be compatible over all firms or for a representative firm (or plan).

Following this interpretation, we could model and compute expected plan benefits using the methodology outlined in 2.3.1 for work life benefits (i.e., expected termination benefit plus expected virtual benefit for entry age 25 tenure 0). Some examples computed on the basis of the data used in this chapter are given in Table 3.1. These correspond to our most probable economic scenario with a long term inflation rate of 4 percent, a real fund rate of return of 2.5 percent, and a wage growth rate of 2 percent.

Observations that can be made on the basis of these results regarding the impacts of mobility, termination rates, and vesting rules, would be substantially the same as the corresponding observations in Chapter 2. Thus mobility has a large impact on plan benefits. By giving rise to unvested terminations and by dividing a longer period of pensionable service in one employment into shorter periods of such service in several employments, mobility causes pension forfeitures and reductions. The former effect applies to all plans, but the latter is relevant only in final average plans where benefits vested for a given year of service are determined by wages earned

TABLE 3.1. Expected Plan Benefits

Mobility	Vesting Rule	25 – 60			25 – 65		
		CA	FA	MP	CA	FA	MP
Low	10	8.37	15.31	11.94	13.66	27.76	21.54
	5	9.01	16.01	12.97	14.50	27.68	23.14
	2	9.28	16.28	13.50	14.87	28.05	23.98
Moderate	10	6.29	10.35	8.68	10.60	18.39	16.11
	5	7.68	11.88	10.75	12.59	20.56	19.47
	2	8.53	12.76	12.26	13.84	21.80	21.96
High	10	3.93	6.00	5.25	6.94	10.98	10.11
	5	5.21	7.94	7.72	9.63	13.91	14.29
	2	7.34	9.57	10.55	12.03	16.20	19.08

in later years in the same employment. Thus these plans are doubly affected by mobility. Also, since reductions in creditable service are more pronounced during younger years when termination rates are higher, MP plans are more sensitive to mobility than CA plans.

Regarding vesting rules, we can see, as before, that the effect on expected plan benefit is marginal for low mobility groups. As termination rates applicable to plan members increase, however, the vesting rule may become critical, especially in CA plans. As noted before, in relation to work life benefits, the relative insensitivity to vesting rules in final average plans is due to the fact that benefits related to different ages in these plans depend heavily on the age of termination. Therefore, a more liberal vesting provision means a smaller percentage increase in benefit, as compared to CA plans, associated with creditable service at different ages. Overall, more stringent vesting provisions are more responsive to plan types and parameters and higher rates of termination magnify this response.

Expected plan benefits for the normal retirement age 65 are much larger than those associated with the early retirement age of 60. For in all plans, more benefit will accrue over a longer period and a further increase in plan benefit will result from a shorter postretirement life expectancy. In addition, if not excluded, plan benefit related to the length of service that terminates with retirement will be larger in FA plans. And, the fund will realize returns for five additional years in MP plans. It can also be seen from the table that the relative increases in expected plan benefits under more liberal vesting rules are nearly the same for both retirement ages. Similarly, higher rates of termination do not appear to have a notable interaction with the retirement age in terms of relative plan benefits in the mean.

So far, the discussion is based on the most probable economic scenario and noncontributory plans. To isolate the effects of inflation and the source of contributions, we have recomputed the expected plan benefits using the most probable (moderate) and high estimates for the rate of inflation in contributory and noncontributory plans. The results are presented in Table 3.2.

The contributory-noncontributory distinction is irrelevant to Table 3.2 in MP plans. In defined benefit plans, increases in expected plan benefit from noncontributory to contributory mode is due to the computation of benefit in contributory plans as the greater of the accrued pension or what the accumulated contributions would buy.[2] These increases are larger for higher rates of termination and inflation, larger in CA plans than in FA plans and larger for the retirement age 65 than for 60.

The results also indicate decreases in expected benefit of about 20 percent from moderate to high rates of inflation in noncontributory CA plans for retirement age 60. These decreases in plan benefit are smaller in con-

TABLE 3.2. Expected Plan Benefits under Different Inflationary Assumptions in Noncontributory and Contributory Plans

Mobil-ity	Vesting Rule	Retirement Age: 65						Retirement Age: 60					
		Non-Contributory			Contributory			Non-Contributory			Contributory		
		CA	FA	MP	CA	FA	MP	CA	FA	MP	CA	FA	MP
Moderate Inflation (4 percent)													
Low	10	13.7	26.8	21.6	14.0	26.9	21.6	8.4	14.3	11.9	8.4	15.3	11.9
	5	14.5	27.7	23.1	15.1	28.1	23.1	9.0	16.0	13.0	9.2	16.1	13.0
	2	14.8	28.1	24.0	15.7	28.7	24.0	9.3	16.3	13.5	9.5	16.5	13.5
Moderate	10	10.6	18.4	16.1	11.0	18.5	16.1	6.3	10.4	8.7	6.4	10.4	8.7
	5	12.6	20.6	19.5	13.4	21.1	19.5	7.7	11 9	10.8	7.9	12.1	10.8
	2	13.8	21.8	22.2	15.2	23.0	22.2	8.6	12.8	12.5	9.0	13.1	12.5
High	10	6.9	11.0	10.0	7.2	11.1	10.0	3.9	6.0	5.3	4.0	6.0	5.3
	5	9.6	13.9	14.3	10.3	14.5	14.3	5.7	7.9	7.7	5.9	8.1	7.7
	2	12.0	16.3	18.4	13.5	17.6	18.4	7.4	9.6	10.2	7.2	9.5	10.2
High Inflation (6 percent)													
Low	10	11.1	25.4	24.3	11.9	25.8	24.3	6.4	13.5	12.5	6.7	13.6	12.3
	5	11.8	26.1	26.1	13.0	26.9	26.1	6.9	14.0	13.5	7.3	14.3	13.5
	2	12.1	26.4	27.0	13.6	27.6	27.0	7.1	14.2	14.1	7.6	14.5	14.1
Mod	10	8.7	17.2	18.1	9.5	17.6	18.1	4.9	9.0	9.1	5.1	9.1	9.1
	5	10.3	19.0	21.9	11.9	20.1	21.9	5.9	10.2	11.2	6.5	10.6	11.2
	2	11.3	19.9	24.7	13.7	22.0	24.7	6.6	10.8	12.8	7.5	11.6	12.8
High	10	5.7	10.1	11.4	7.3	10.5	11.4	3.1	5.2	5.5	3.2	5.2	5.5
	5	7.9	12.6	16.1	9.3	13.7	16.1	4.4	6.7	8.1	4.9	7.0	8.1
	2	9.9	14.5	20.9	12.7	17.0	20.9	5.7	7.9	10.8	6.7	8.8	10.8

tributory plans and for the retirement age 65. More stringent vesting rules and higher rates of termination do not appear to aggravate the impact of inflation. As expected, reductions in benefit due to inflation are considerably less in FA plans than in CA plans. In contrast to defined benefit plans, expected plan benefit increases in MP plans together with the rate of inflation. This is due to the relatively cheaper annuities purchased at retirement.

3.2.2 Expected Plan Costs

Theoretically, the cost of plan benefits is the amount of money needed to pay for these benefits during the retirement period. A plan is said to be fully funded if at the time of the retirement of a group of workers, money is available in the fund to cover all of their retirement benefits. This concept is somewhat more complicated in practice, however, because of the age-tenure mix of the active employees. In actuarial analysis, the cost of a pension plan is generally established by relating the future benefits for all workers to the payroll received by all workers. In essence, this approach is an aggregation across age cohorts. We will take a more specific view in that we will regard a plan fully funded if the retirement benefits due to a given age cohort could be paid out of the withholdings from their wages and/or contributions made on their behalf during their working years. This restriction is not sufficient, however, to determine a unique cost method. For simplicity, we chose an approach that expresses the pension cost as a constant fraction of the wage rate received by a worker during his or her entire career. This costing method is similar to the *projected benefit cost method with constant share*.[3]

Following this approach, we first define the *plan cost* as *plan benefit* times the cost of unit annuity purchased at retirement times the conditional probability of survival to retirement. In symbols:

$$C(a,T) = B(a,T) \ A \ (r,T) \ L(a,T).$$

Here, $C(a,T)$ is the plan cost that depends on the beginning age, a, of a typical work life and the retirement age T. $B(a,T)$ is the plan benefit introduced above; $A(r,T)$ is the cost of unit annuity purchased at retirement which depends on the retirement age and the interest rate assumption r; and, $L(a,T)$ is the probability that the individual will be alive at age T, given that he or she was alive at age a. Note that the way it is constructed, this relationship relates more naturally to the work life perspective of Chapter 2; however, it is also meaningful for the plan perspective under our "compatibility" assumption. Another way of stating this assumption would be to say that with respect to pension accrual, a representative firm would be indifferent, on the average, between replacing or hiring back a terminating employee.

Given r, a and T, in the above relationship between plan costs and benefits, $A(r,T)$ and $L(a,T)$ are constants. Under our moderate economic scenario, the inflation and real return rates of 0.04 and 0.025, imply a nominal interest rate of $(1+.04) (1+.025) - 1 = 0.066$. Using this rate and the mortality tables, we have determined the cost of a $1 annuity purchased at the normal retirement age as $9.47 and early retirement age as $10.72. Also, the conditional probabilities of survival to the early and normal retirement ages, given the individual is alive at age 25, are 0.838 and 0.760, respectively. On this basis, the relationship between plan benefit and plan cost would be: $C(25,65) = 7.20 \ B(25,65)$ for the normal retirement age, and $C(25,60) = 8.98 \ B(25,60)$ for the early retirement age. Therefore, plan cost is proportional to plan benefit. Since plan benefit is expressed as a fraction of the age at retirement, the plan cost is also expressed in terms of that wage.

The cost of a noncontributory pension plan *as a fraction of the wage* in any given year can be expressed as the ratio of the plan cost to the value $V(a,T)$ of life time wages corrected for mortality. Thus $V(a,T)$ is the expected invested value, at the assumed interest rate, of all wages earned over the work life defined by the parameters a and T. The expectation is taken with respect to probabilities of survival. That is, an individual will receive the projected wage during a certain year if he or she is alive at that time. Consequently, the cost rate for noncontributory plans can be expressed as $c(a,T) = C(a,T)/V(a,T)$. This specifies the pension costs as a *level percentage of the payroll*.

Determination of the cost rates for contributory plans must take into account the reimbursements of their own contributions to employees who terminate prior to vesting and to employees who die prior to retirement. Denote these quantities by G_r and G_d. A third reimbursement, applicable to defined benefit plans, arises if the excess contributions are returned to the employees when their own contributions buy more than the defined benefit. Let this reimbursement be represented by G_e. The cost rate in contributory plans can now be expressed as $c(a,T) = [C(a,T) + G_r + G_d + G_e]/V(a,T)$. In addition, if v is the employee contribution rate, then the employer cost rate is $c(a,T) - v$ and the employee cost rate is $v - (G_r + G_d + G_e)/V(a,T)$.

As examples, we present in Table 3.3 the total cost rate (employer cost plus employee cost in contributory plans), expressed as a level percentage of the payroll in any given year. As expected, costs are higher under lower rates of termination, more liberal vesting rules, contributory plans, final average (as compared to career average) plans, and under the early retirement age 60. It is also seen that the cost rates decrease with increasing inflation in defined benefit plans. As noted earlier, although wages increase with inflation, vested benefits related to terminated employments do not in defined benefit plans. On the other hand, it is cheaper to maintain a constant level of benefit during postretirement years when the interest rates are high. The results also show that the expected relative cost increases in moving to more liberal vesting rules are larger in CA plans than in FA plans, in noncontributory than in contributory defined benefit plans, and for the retirement age 60 than for 65. In many cases, however, cost differentials under alternative vesting rules are rather small.

3.3 VARIABILITY AND DISTRIBUTION OF PLAN BENEFITS AND COSTS

In addition to expected values, variability of costs and benefits is also of interest for a number of reasons. For one thing, how representative the mean is depends on how small the variance is relative to the mean. In Table

TABLE 3.3. Expected Plan Costs (Employer plus Employee Costs) as a Constant Fraction of the Payroll

| Mobil-ity | Vesting Rule | Retirement Age: 65 | | | | | | Retirement Age: 60 | | | | | |
| | | Non-Contributory | | | Contributory | | | Non-Contributory | | | Contributory | | |
		CA	FA	MP	CA	FA	MP	CA	FA	MP	CA	FA	MP
				Moderate Inflation (4 percent)									
Low	10	2.8	5.4	4.4	3.4	6.0	5.1	3.2	5.8	4.6	3.7	6.3	5.2
	5	2.9	5.6	4.7	3.5	6.1	5.3	3.4	6.1	5.0	3.8	6.5	5.4
	2	3.0	5.7	4.9	3.5	6.1	5.4	3.5	6.2	5.2	3.9	6.5	5.5
Moderate	10	2.2	3.7	3.3	3.2	4.7	4.6	2.4	4.0	3.3	3.4	5.0	4.6
	5	2.6	4.2	4.0	3.4	5.0	4.9	2.9	4.5	4.1	3.7	5.3	5.0
	2	2.8	4.4	4.4	3.5	5.1	5.1	3.3	4.9	4.7	3.8	5.4	5.2
High	10	1.4	2.3	2.1	2.9	3.7	4.0	1.5	2.3	2.0	3.1	3.8	4.0
	5	2.0	2.8	2.9	3.2	4.0	4.4	2.2	3.0	2.9	3.4	4.2	4.4
	2	2.4	3.3	3.8	3.4	4.3	4.7	2.8	3.5	3.9	3.6	4.5	4.7
				High Inflation (6 percent)									
Low	10	2.0	4.6	4.4	2.6	5.1	5.1	2.4	4.9	4.6	2.9	5.4	5.2
	5	2.1	4.7	4.7	2.7	5.2	5.3	2.5	5.1	5.0	3.0	5.5	5.4
	2	2.2	4.7	4.9	2.7	5.3	5.4	2.6	5.2	5.2	3.0	5.5	5.5
Moderate	10	1.6	3.1	3.3	2.7	4.1	4.6	1.8	3.3	3.3	2.8	4.3	4.6
	5	1.9	3.4	4.0	2.8	4.3	4.9	2.2	3.7	4.1	3.0	4.5	5.0
	2	2.0	3.6	4.4	2.9	4.4	5.1	2.4	3.9	4.7	3.1	4.6	5.2
High	10	1.0	1.8	2.1	2.6	3.3	4.0	1.1	1.9	2.0	2.7	3.4	4.0
	5	1.4	2.3	2.9	2.8	3.6	4.4	1.6	2.5	2.9	2.9	3.7	4.4
	2	1.8	2.6	3.7	2.9	3.7	4.7	2.1	2.9	3.8	3.1	3.9	4.7

3.4, we present the coefficients of variation of plan benefits under the same scenarios as in Table 3.1. Coefficient of variation is defined as the ratio of the standard deviation to the mean; it is thus a relative measure of dispersion. The measure is independent of the benefit level in defined benefit plans; that is, the same numerical values would have resulted if higher or lower levels of benefit were used in computations. Similarly, the measure does not depend on the particular contribution level used in the money purchase plan. Consequently, as opposed to the means, coefficients of variation under defined benefit plans are directly comparable with those under the money purchase plan.

It is important to note what kind of variability is being measured here. There are two major sources of variability that affect plan benefits and costs, as these quantities are defined. The first is related to mobility, the second is to economic variables (inflation, wage growth, rate of return). Since we assumed away the second kind of variability by making specific assumptions about the economic variables, the variability we are measuring

TABLE 3.4. Coefficients of Variation of Plan Benefits and Costs

Mobility	Vesting Rule	25 - 60			25 - 65		
		CA	FA	MP	CA	FA	MP
Low	10	.24	.33	.23	.21	.32	.20
	5	.11	.25	.11	.10	.26	.10
	2	.05	.23	.05	.05	.24	.05
Moderate	10	.51	.61	.49	.45	.57	.43
	5	.26	.41	.25	.23	.41	.23
	2	.13	.32	.12	.11	.34	.10
High	10	.89	.99	.86	.79	.91	.76
	5	.47	.62	.46	.42	.59	.41
	2	.22	.41	.21	.20	.42	.19

in Table 3.4 is induced primarily by the variable lengths of service. Secondly, two different quantities are being represented by what we called the plan benefit. The first is the ultimate benefit to be derived by a typical individual from his or her career membership in pension plans, from age 25 to age 60 or 65. This is in keeping with the work life perspective of Chapter 2. The second quantity being represented is the projection over the comparable time span (i.e., 35 or 40 years) of benefits accruing to different incumbents of a typical employment position. This is along the plan perspective of this chapter. As we pointed out earlier, the two quantities must be the same, on the average, if the plan or the firm is representative of the industry under consideration. Thus variability in plan benefits is the variability in total benefits attributable to time spans that correspond to typical work lives.

We have seen above that the plan cost can be expressed as a constant times the plan benefit. (The constant was estimated to be 7.20 for the retirement age of 65 and 8.98 for the retirement age of 60.) Recall also that in this representation, both the plan benefit and the plan cost are expressed in terms of the replacement rate at the respective retirement age. It then follows that the mean plan cost is this applicable constant times the mean plan benefit, and similarly for the standard deviation of plan costs. Consequently, since the coefficient of variation is the ratio of the mean to standard deviation, it remains the same from plan benefits to plan costs. Relative variabilities given in Table 3.4 then also apply to plan costs. Note, however, that the subject is only the noncontributory plans as corrections for returned employee contributions have not been made. Also, the cost measure is not in terms of a percentage of payroll, as the value of wages is not brought into the picture.

An examination of Table 3.4 shows that the relative variability decreases as the vesting rule is made more liberal. It is also evident that the vesting rule has a substantial impact on the variability of costs and benefits, variability that is induced, as we remarked above, by employee mobility. The highest level of variability is exhibited by FA plans. The MP and CA plans appear nearly identical.[4] This high dispersion of benefits and costs in FA plans can again be explained by the fact that in these plans benefits associated with a creditable year of service may vary substantially as a function of the time of employment termination, because of wage growth in the current job.

Due to the random nature of the employment termination process, plan benefit and cost are random variables. Therefore, their full description requires the construction of their probability distributions. The information provided by the mean and variance would be sufficient for some but not other purposes. They do not, for example, provide any information about the outliers in terms of the proportions of recipients with very low or very high benefit levels, or equivalently, the probabilities with which the plan cost would be high or low.

Cumulative distributions of plan benefits for retirement age 65 are presented in Figure 3.1, Figure 3.2 and Figure 3.3, under different vesting rules, plan types, and termination rates.[5] Again, through the work life interpretation, these would also represent the distribution of work life pension benefits accruing over a 40-year period from age 25 to age 65. By a simple scaling of the horizontal axes by 7.20, these distributions also apply to pension costs. As we have seen above, plan benefit and plan cost are related to each other by this constant.

For every benefit (or cost) level on the horizontal axes, the graphs determine the proportion of times the plan benefit (or cost) will be *below* this level. (From the work life perspective, the reference would be to the proportion of recipients below a certain benefit level.) For example, we can see from Figure 3.2 that the plan benefit in FA (5 years) plans under high mobility and the cliff-10 vesting rule will be less than 15 (15 percent of the retirement wage) for about 68 percent of the time (or, 68 percent of the high mobility employees will receive less than 15). This frequency reduces to about 10 percent under low mobility. By implication, the plan benefit will be more than 15 with probability 0.32 and 0.90, respectively (or, 32 percent and 90 percent, respectively, of the high and low mobility workers will receive more than 15). Conversely, by identifying first the percentages, one can determine the percentiles of the distributions. Again from Figure 3.2, the first quartiles under the cliff-10 rule, and high and low rates of mobility, are 3.5 and 15, respectively. Also, medians are 10 and 20, third quartiles are 17.5 and 35, and interquartile ranges are 14 and 20. Thus plan benefits in the middle 50 percent will vary from 3.5 to 17.5 if termination rates are high, but from 15 to 35 if termination rates are low. Note that the

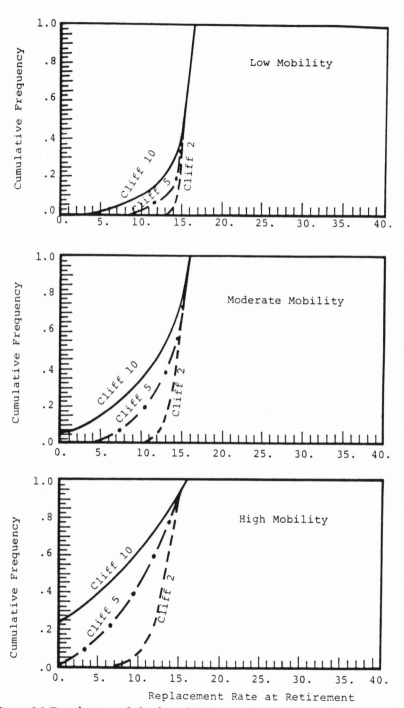

Figure 3.1 Distributions of plan benefit (plan cost) in career average plans under different cliff vesting rules

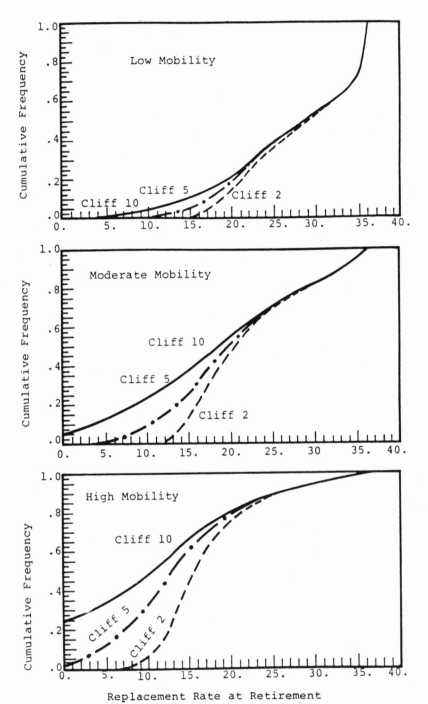

Figure 3.2 Distributions of plan benefit (plan cost) in final five years' average plans under different cliff vesting rules

maximum possible benefit is 36 and that 25 percent of the low mobility employees will receive more than 35 under any vesting rule.

The results show that the impact of vesting rules in defined benefit plans is marginal when termination rates are low. This impact becomes substantial for moderate and high mobility groups. In general, distributions shift to the right as the vesting rule becomes more liberal, thus placing smaller fractions of recipients below a given benefit level. The vesting rule is much more influential in the money purchase plan (Figure 3.3). Even modest changes in the service requirement for vesting seem to create significant shifts in distributions of benefits and costs. This is a direct consequence of the periods of service during which benefits are forfeited due to termination before the vesting requirements are met. As pointed out before, in terms of their value at retirement, such benefits are comparable for comparable lengths of service in money purchase plans. Their forfeiture, therefore, would induce a corresponding decrease in plan benefits. In comparison, in defined benefit plans, benefits forfeited at younger years would have a relatively minor impact on the purchasing power of the pension income at retirement, as termination benefits are not indexed to inflation.

The impact of mobility is substantial in all cases, as reflected by a shift to the left in distributions from low to high levels. This is due to the fact that as termination rates increase, the proportion of plan benefits below a given level would also increase, thus placing relatively larger fractions of recipients with little or no pension income in higher termination sectors. For example, from the work life perspective, 27.5 percent of the highly mobile employees would have no vested pension under the cliff-10 rule. This proportion drops to about 2.5 percent under the cliff-5 rule. The same proportions with moderate mobility are 7 percent under the cliff-10 vesting rule and negligible or zero under the other two rules. Consequently, as a measure of the risk of terminating employees, probability of no vested pension is highly sensitive to vesting rules and termination rates.

Regarding the impact of the plan type, it is seen that the maximum possible benefit is 16 in CA plans, 36 in FA (5-year) plans and 25 in the MP plans.[6] Narrowness of the benefit range in CA plans is coupled with a significant concentration of the frequency near the upper range. In contrast, the range of the distributions for FA plans are very wide. The fact remains, however, that FA plans yield higher costs and benefits than CA plans. According to Figure 3.2, for example, the probability that the plan benefit is more than 16 in a FA plan under low mobility and a 10-year vesting rule is 0.88, while 16 is the maximum benefit level in a CA plan even under full and immediate vesting.

Distribution of plan benefits would be the most uniform under CA plans. At the other extreme are the FA plans, with the MP plans falling somewhere in between. But this uniformity is only with respect to the manifestation of mobility induced variability. Clearly, the cost of a defined benefit

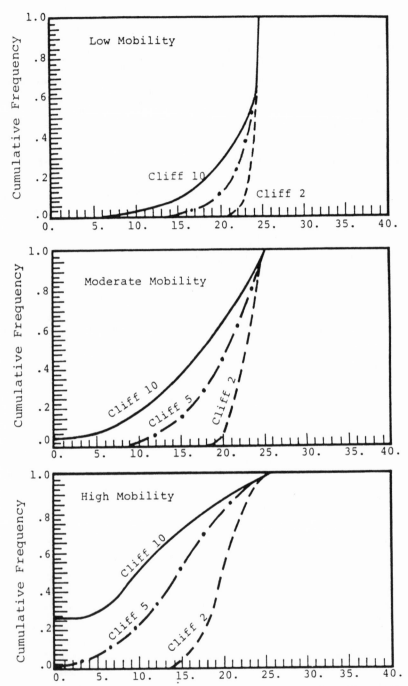

Figure 3.3 Distributions of plan benefit (plan cost) in money purchase plans under different cliff vesting rules

plan would also fluctuate with economic conditions, as the cost of annuity depends on the prevailing rate of return on investment. On the other hand, while featuring a mobility induced variability that is more comparable to CA plans than to FA plans, the cost to the firm of a MP plan has an upper bound that is implied by the rate of contribution. Thus in terms of the variation and predictability of costs, MP plans offer a clear advantage for employers.

In terms of the efficient allocation of labor, from the firm's perspective, it is clear that CA plans would place the lowest restriction on mobility, by virtue of the comparatively lower and more uniform level of plan benefit. At the other extreme are the final average plans with short averaging periods. Also, in terms of the impact of regulation through statutory vesting rules, CA and MP plans appear more sensitive but FA plans are relatively neutral to these provisions. This distinction all but disappears, however, if termination rates applicable to plan members are low.

3.4 SOME RECENT ISSUES—A CASE STUDY

In this and the following section, we discuss a number of recent issues on the basis of the concepts and measures we established so far. This discussion is organized in two case studies that are adopted from the research work performed for the Government of Ontario.[7] The two cases feature two different modes of analysis: (1) a "steady state" analysis of the pension benefit and pension cost differentials induced by a number of changes in a pension plan or a pension system; and (2) a "dynamic" analysis of describing the evolution of pension benefits and pension costs as these changes take effect. This section is devoted to the steady state analysis.

In 1981, a number of policy initiatives were being examined by the Ontario government as central elements of a pension reform package. These initiatives were directed mainly to defined benefit plans. In addition to earlier vesting, which we considered in considerable detail before, these included: (1) the use of realistic interest rates on withdrawn employee contributions in contributory defined benefit plans; (2) payment by the employer contributions for at least one-half of the pension benefit in contributory defined benefit plans; (3) adjustment through excess interest of pension benefits in payment; and (4) adjustment through excess interest of deferred pension benefits. These potential changes in the pension system were examined in detail in a comparative setting as they are added to the "reform package" sequentially.

The study was conducted under a set of assumptions that are similar to the ones outlined in Section 3.1. In particular, plan types and decremental assumptions were the same. In this section we will restrict ourselves to defined benefit plans. Beginning of the work life was represented by age

20, rather than 25; however, this has a relatively minor impact on the results, especially in the case of defined benefit plans. The rate of inflation was represented by a range of values that included the moderate (4 percent) and high (6 percent) levels used above. The real wage growth rate was again 2 percent but, instead of a fixed 2.5 percent real interest rate, two different real rate of return assumptions were used: low (1 percent) and high (3 percent).

The pension cost implications of the four reform initiatives listed above were examined in a sequential and comparative setting. Although the original study included pension benefits also, here we restrict ourselves to pension costs, measured in terms of a constant fraction of wage over the work life for employers and employees. In order to provide a basis of comparison, we first look at the pension costs under full vesting after 5 years of service and the assumption that on termination before vesting, employee contributions in contributory plans are returned with *no interest*. The results are shown in Table 3.5. Entries under "Total Cost" are the expected pension costs in noncontributory plans. Entries under "Employer Cost" are the employer's shares of the expected plan costs in contributory plans. The differences would then be employee costs net of returned contributions in contributory plans. Under low rate of return, low inflation and

TABLE 3.5. Pension Costs under Base Scenarios°

| | | Real Interest Rate = 0.01 | | | | Real Interest Rate = 0.03 | | | |
| | | Total Cost | | Employer Cost | | Total Cost | | Employer Cost | |
Infla-tion	Mobil-ity	CA	FA	CA	FA	CA	FA	CA	FA
.04	Low	4.03	8.26	1.86	6.08	2.35	4.82	.27	2.69
	Mod.	3.55	6.05	1.66	4.15	2.07	3.53	.34	1.74
	High	2.74	4.05	1.28	2.57	1.60	2.36	.27	.99
.06	Low	2.85	6.82	.73	4.65	1.68	4.03	-.36	1.93
	Mod.	2.52	4.87	.71	3.01	1.49	2.88	-.18	1.15
	High	1.96	3.19	.56	1.75	1.16	1.89	-.11	.57

°Full vesting after 5 years of service and no interest on returned employee contributions.

low mobility, for example, the total cost in a CA plan is 4.03 percent of the payroll, while the employer cost is 1.86 percent. The employee cost in contributory plans would therefore be 4.03 − 1.86 = 2.17 percent. Since the employee contributions in defined benefit plans is taken as 2.5 percent, the difference of 0.33 percent represents returned contributions. If returned contributions are viewed as additional benefits paid out of the pension fund, then the total cost, including returned contributions, would be 4.03 + 0.33 = 4.3 percent of the payroll.

It is seen that most of the plan cost in contributory plans are met by employee contributions. Negative entries under CA plans mean that under those circumstances, employee contributions would be more than sufficient to pay for the plan benefits. This is clearly a consequence of the assumption that on termination before vesting, employee contributions are returned with no interest. At the time the study was conducted, whether a terminating employee received interest on his or her returned contributions depended on the terms of the plan. It was not uncommon for employees to receive interest at a very low rate or no interest at all.

3.4.1 Returned Employee Contributions and Cost Sharing in Contributory Plans

Clearly, adding interest to returned contributions to employees who terminate before vesting at the amount a person could get in the market place will mean an additional cost to the employer. To measure this, we computed the employer cost under the assumption that interest at the assumed fund rate of return is added to employee reimbursements following unvested exits from contributory plans. The results are shown in Table 3.6. In spite of rather substantial increases in employer costs, more than half of the pension costs in CA plans are still met by employee contributions in almost all the cases examined. The situation is quite different for FA plans where the employer share of the plan cost was substantial to begin with. Still, there are important cost increases throughout, especially under the high rate of return assumption. It may be surprising to see that the employer's costs would increase as much as they do, just on the basis of adding interest at a realistic rate to withdrawn employee contributions. Even then, the employer's share of the cost is less than that of the employee's in CA plans.

The rationale for equal cost allocation is a reflection of the understanding that most employees have in contributory defined benefit plans. This understanding is that "the pension is paid for by a percentage deducted from the employee's wages *and a matching contribution* made by the employer."[8] Payment by the employer of at least an equal share of the cost recognizes this understanding. It also reinforces the modern view of pen-

TABLE 3.6. Employer Costs in Contributory Plans° under Improved Employee Reimbursements† (Reform 1) and Equal Cost Allocation‡ (Reform 2)

		Real Interest Rate = 0.01				Real Interest Rate = 0.03			
		Total Cost		Employer Cost		Total Cost		Employer Cost	
Infla-tion	Mobil-ity	CA	FA	CA	FA	CA	FA	CA	FA
.04	Low	2.09	6.27	.72	3.05	2.32	6.40	1.51	3.25
	Mod.	1.91	4.36	.84	2.16	2.21	4.56	1.41	2.44
	High	1.52	2.79	.74	1.40	1.78	2.98	1.12	1.66
.06	Low	1.09	4.93	.40	2.40	1.71	5.09	1.24	2.56
	Mod.	1.13	3.34	.55	1.70	1.61	3.58	1.15	1.94
	High	.95	2.08	.51	1.10	1.29	2.31	.90	1.33

°Employee contributions are assumed to be 2.5 percent.
†Interest at the fund rate (inflation rate plus real interest rate) is added to withdrawn employee contributions on terminations before vesting.
‡Employer pays for at least one half of the plan benefit; excess employee contributions are returned with interest.

sions as a form of deferred wages. Expected cost increases under the provision that the employer pay for at least one half the plan benefit are also shown in Table 3.6. Again, CA plans are affected more substantially.

3.4.2 Indexation of Benefits—Excess Interest Adjustments

In relation to reform initiatives 4 and 5, the method of "excess interest" was used to provide for a degree of inflation adjustment in pensions in payment to retired employees in all plans, deferred pensions payable to terminated employees in defined benefit plans, and accrued benefits of active employees in CA plans. This approach to pension benefit adjustment had received some attention prior to the conduct of the original study.[9] It is directed to increasing benefits by a percentage corresponding to interest earned in excess of an anticipated or prescribed *base rate* which is an approximation to what is perceived to be the real rate of interest. While this approach would preserve to some extent the relative positions of both the employees and the fund (or the employer) against changes in the rate of inflation, if all earnings in excess of the base rate are used to increase benefits, the fund management would have no incentive to achieve the highest return possible. This moral hazard problem is solved by choosing a second index, the *guide rate*, that represents the expected performance of the fund. This rate is to be determined exogenously to the fund. Thus the employee would see his or her pension benefit adjusted by the difference between the two rates, and the firm or the insurer managing the fund would benefit or not depending on the performance of the fund with respect to the guide rate.

Considerations related to the proper choice and implementation of the two rates of adjustment were outside the scope of the original study. A base rate of 3.5 percent was used in respect of benefits arising from service after the effective date of the reform initiatives.[10] This level represents a commonly used assumption in funding pension plans and valuing life insurance benefits. Although it would not have as severe an effect on funding as would a lower rate, a prescribed base rate of 3.5 percent was considered as being rather on the high side as an approximation for the real rate of interest. It was therefore decided to represent the real fund rate of interest separately in calculations from the base rate and an average of 2 percent was considered more realistic for the fund rate. The alternative assumptions of 3 and 1 percent for the real rate of interest were introduced in this context to examine the relative impact of superior and inferior performance. This decoupling of the real interest rate and the base rate is inconsistent with the premise that the base rate should represent the rate of return that would exist were there no inflation. It is not inconsistent, however, with the objective that the base rate should be prescribed at a level high enough to minimize potential difficulties in funding.

As a transitional provision, a modified base rate of 7 percent was used in calculations to adjust benefits related to service prior to the effective date of the reform initiatives.[11] The rationale behind a transitional base rate was that while the long term objective should be to use a single base rate for all benefits, if such a requirement is imposed at the outset on all accrued as well as future benefits, it would create immediately a large unfunded liability in most pension plans. On the other hand, avoiding any retroactivity was considered undesirable as the build-up of benefits from future service and the effect of an inflation adjustment limited to such service would be slow to develop. The 7 percent level was based on the observation that this would not create any serious unfunded liability as few plans were funded at that time under the assumption of interest rates over 7 percent.

In all cases, the guide rate, R_g, is specified in the analyses below as a function of the assumed rate of inflation, I, according to the relationship: $1 + R_g$ = 1.02(1+I). This is consistent with the average real interest rate assumption of 2 percent for pension funds. (In practice, this rate could be established by reference to an index of current market rates.) In relation to the use of the modified base rate of 7 percent, no negative adjustments were made in calculations if the guide rate fell below 7 percent due to low inflation. In practice, if the guide rate falls below the base rate, it would be normal and desirable to adjust the benefits downward. As an example, if the inflation rate is 8 percent, the guide rate would be approximately 10 percent. Future benefits should therefore be increased by 6.5 percent (i.e., 10 − 3.5). The real rate of return assumptions of 3 and 1 percent then imply net earnings of 4.5 and 2.5 percent (i.e., 8+3 − 6.5 = 4.5).

Expected pension cost rates, again expressed in terms of a fixed fraction of payroll, under the excess interest adjustment of benefits in payment and deferred benefits are given in Table 3.7. (Note that the reform initiatives are incorporated in a cumulative setting.) An examination of this table

TABLE 3.7. Expected Pension Costs under the Excess Interest Adjustment of Benefits in Payment (Reform 3) and Deferred Benefits (Reform 4)

| Infla-tion | Mobil-ity | Real Interest Rate = 0.01 | | | | Real Interest Rate = 0.03 | | | |
| | | Total Cost | | Employer Cost | | Total Cost | | Employer Cost | |
		CA	FA	CA	FA	CA	FA	CA	FA
				Reforms 1, 2, and 3[1]					
.04	Low	4.91	10.07	3.12	8.15	2.81	5.76	1.73	4.13
	Mod.	4.32	7.38	2.89	5.81	2.47	4.22	1.64	3.05
	High	3.34	4.93	2.29	3.79	1.91	2.82	1.31	2.05
.06	Low	3.98	9.52	2.35	7.71	2.27	5.44	1.50	3.91
	Mod.	3.52	6.80	2.28	5.39	2.01	3.89	1.42	2.85
	High	2.74	4.46	1.86	3.46	1.56	2.55	1.13	1.89
				Reforms 1, 2, 3 and 4					
.04	Low	6.94	10.59	4.92	8.56	3.97	6.06	2.31	4.27
	Mod.	6.05	8.11	4.32	6.37	3.46	4.64	2.19	3.25
	High	4.61	5.60	3.32	4.30	2.64	3.20	1.73	2.23
.06	Low	7.04	10.29	5.02	8.27	4.02	5.88	2.35	4.11
	Mod.	6.14	7.90	4.41	6.15	3.51	4.51	2.22	3.13
	High	4.67	5.46	3.38	4.16	2.67	3.12	1.76	2.16

[1]For Reforms 1 and 2, see Table 3.6.

shows that the excess interest adjustments of benefits in payment, over and above the two reform initiatives considered before, would increase the total pension costs by about 20 percent under the moderate and 40 percent under the high inflationary assumption. Also, the employer costs in FA plans would increase by about 25 percent and 50 percent, respectively. These increases are insensitive to mobility and the real interest rate assumptions being used. On the other hand, employer costs in CA plans appear to depend on all the variables. These increases vary from 14 percent under the low mobility, low inflation, high real return scenario to 53 percent under the high mobility, high inflation, low real return scenario.

Increases in cost from the indexation of benefits in payment to the indexation of deferred benefits are the most substantial in CA plans. Total cost increases range from about 40 percent under moderate inflation to 75 percent under low inflation. These increases are independent of the real interest rate and change only slightly with mobility. Employer cost increases in CA plans vary from 30 to 100 percent, depending on inflation, rate of return and mobility. Cost increases in FA plans are much lower, with a range of 5 to 22 percent in total costs and 3 to 20 percent in employer costs.

3.5 DYNAMICS OF PENSION REFORM— ANOTHER CASE STUDY

During 1981, there was also the additional concern, on the part of the government policymakers in Ontario and of other parties interested in pension reform, about the length of time it would take for any legislative reform to become effective in delivering improved benefits. How would pension benefits evolve in time as a given "reform package" takes effect? What would be the unfunded liabilities created by these initiatives? In order to respond to these and similar questions, the accrual of benefits and costs were investigated in a dynamic setting. In this investigation, the impact of a given reform package on pension benefits was measured by the evolution of the replacement rate at retirement for cohorts who were of various ages at the time of the effective date of these changes. The dynamics of pension costs was analyzed by computing the liabilities generated by a reform package as a constant-share contribution over the remaining work life for each age cohort. For already retired workers, percentage increases needed in the fund to pay for additional benefits were determined.

The analysis was performed for CA, FA and MP plans, under the assumptions of Section 3.4, relative to the reform initiatives introduced at the beginning of Section 3.4. In addition, replacement of the statutory vesting Rule of 45 and 10 with full vesting after 5 years of service was a high-priority initiative. Based on these, three policy alternatives were formulated: (1) all reforms are introduced at the same time; (2) a partial reform package, made up of earlier vesting, realistic interest rates on returned employee contributions, and the payment by the employer of at least one-half of the cost of benefits in contributory defined benefit plans, is introduced; and (3) a follow-up reform package, involving the excess interest adjustment of benefits, is introduced some time after the introduction of the second alternative. This section is confined to a discussion of the third alternative, under the high real interest rate assumption, as it relates to benefits of active employees and deferred benefits of terminated employees in defined benefit plans. Patterns of evolution of pension benefits and costs in defined benefit plans under the first alternative were generally similar to those under the third alternative.[12]

3.5.1 Evolution of Benefits

Evolution of pension benefits for active employees and deferred benefits for terminated employees in CA plans under the excess interest adjustments is given in Figure 3.4. Plots are the replacement rates under different mobility and inflationary assumptions for cohorts from 20 to 65 years of age at the time the "reform" is initiated. Since individuals just entering the work force will be fully affected by the reform, the initial values represent "steady state" pension benefits under the change. By this we mean the pension benefit that would accrue if the individual were subject to the same set of rules and parameters, including the excess interest adjustments in question, throughout his or her work life. From the plan perspective, this would be the plan benefit examined earlier under the excess interest adjustment of deferred benefits and benefits of active employees. Similarly, terminal values (for age 65) are the "steady state" benefits that would obtain without inflation indexation, but under the initiatives of policy alternative (2) above. (Cost of these benefits are given in Table 3.6.) Clearly, terminal values are benefits that are projected to accrue on behalf of those retiring just before the introduction of the reform; their replacement rates at retirement will not be affected. Intermediate values in the plots are the expected replacement rates at retirement for cohorts that are affected by the reform during a part of their working lives.

Read from right to left, Figure 3.4 describes the changes in pension benefits in CA plans as the reform initiative takes effect. Suppose that the indexation of benefits is instituted starting at time 0. Pension benefits of those who retire just before this time are given by the applicable terminal value for "Age at Reform" 65. Pension benefits of those who retire at time 1 are read under "Age of Reform" 64. In general, the expected replacement

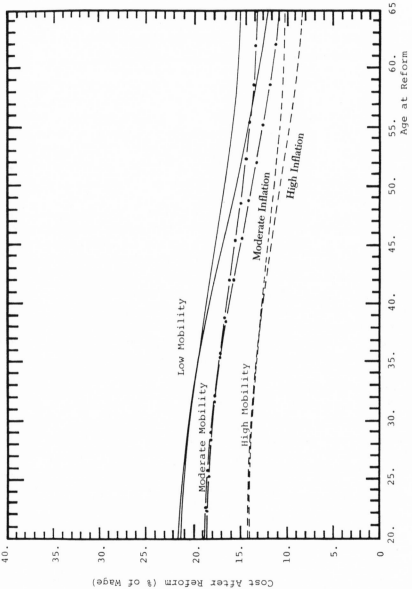

Figure 3.4 Evolution of pension benefits in career average plans

rate for the age cohort retiring n years after the inception of the reform is given under "Age of Reform" 65−n.

Regarding the methodology used in affecting the excess interest adjustments in a dynamic setting, three different cases were considered depending on the timing of an employment termination. First, if the employment is started and terminated after the change, the accrued benefit was indexed by using the base rate of 3.5 percent. Second, if the employment is started before but terminated after the change, the benefit accruing from the years of service following the change was indexed by using the base rate of 3.5 percent, but the benefit accruing from the years of service prior to the introduction of the reform was indexed by using the base rate of 7 percent, starting from the time of change. Finally, if the employment was terminated before the change, the deferred benefit was indexed by using the base rate of 7 percent, starting from the time of change. In all cases, excess interest adjustments were made on a yearly basis in CA plans, both for active and terminated employees.[13]

Evolution of pension benefits in final 5 years' average plans under the excess interest adjustment of benefits to active employees and deferred benefits to terminated employees is presented in Figure 3.5. In these plans, excess interest adjustments were affected only for terminated employees. In view of our assumption that wages grow at the rate of the inflation plus the real wage growth rate, if applied to active employees, excess interest adjustments would have resulted in double indexation. In addition, if a pensionable employment started before but terminated after the reform, part of the accrued benefit, obtained by applying the last 5 years' average wage to the length of service prior to the change, was indexed by using the base rate of 7 percent; and, the rest of the accrued benefit, obtained by applying the same average wage to the length of service after the change, was indexed by using the base rate of 3.5 percent.

According to the above findings, under the excess interest adjustment of deferred benefits, plan benefits would increase by about 0.2 per year in CA plans and 0.1 per year in final 5 years' average plans. It should be noted that these increases as well as the benefits themselves are expressed in terms of replacement rates at retirement. Under the high inflationary assumption, for example, although replacement rates are lower, the dollar value of benefits would be higher due to a higher rate of wage growth resulting in a higher wage at retirement.

3.5.2 Evolution of Pension Costs

Rather than looking at the evolution of pension costs for the aggregate of all age cohorts, evolution of pension costs was examined on the basis of the liabilities generated by a reform initiative as a constant-share contribution

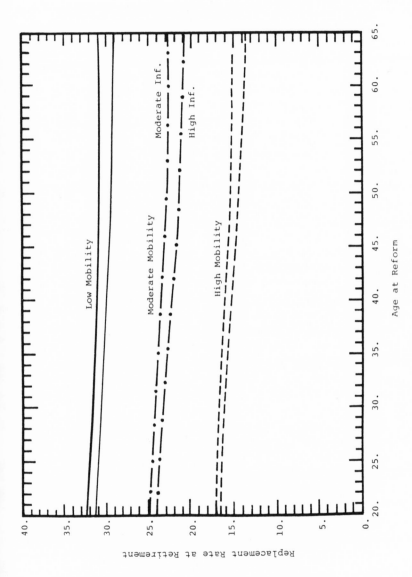

Figure 3.5 Evolution of pension benefits in final average plans

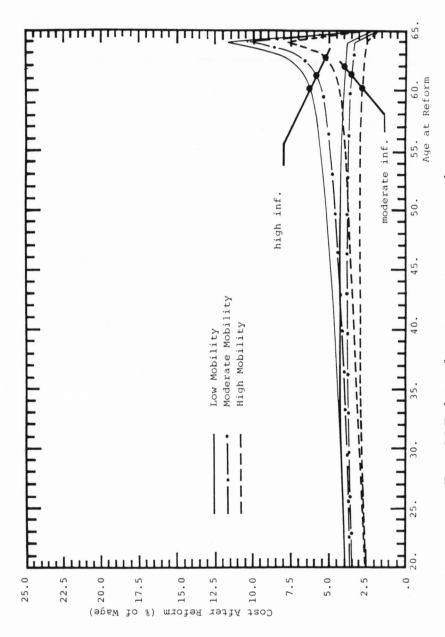

Figure 3.6 Evolution of pension costs in career average plans

108

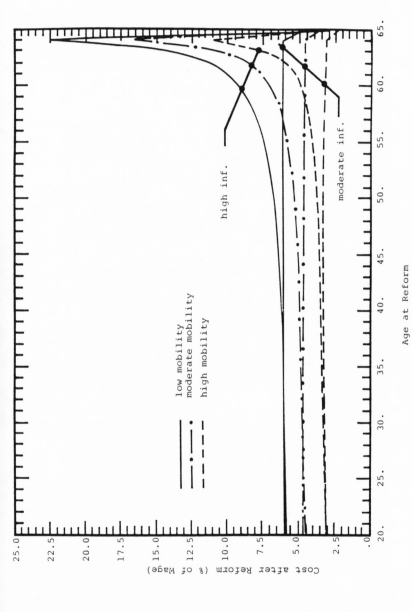

Figure 3.7 Evolution of pension costs in final average plans

109

over the remaining years of work of each age cohort. Results for CA and FA plans are presented in Figure 3.6 and Figure 3.7, respectively. Sharp increases that peak at "Age of Reform" 64 result from shorter periods of time left from the inception of the reform to the time of retirement of older age cohorts. According to the costing method used, increased benefits due to an age cohort are paid out of the withholdings from their wages and/or contributions made on their behalf during their remaining working years.

It appears that it would be practically impossible to subsidize the additional benefits of older workers through their own contributions or contributions made in their behalf. Taken in themselves, serious unfunded liabilities would result with regard to cohorts that are close to retirement at the time of the inception of the reform. The methodology on which these findings are based thus provides a framework for the measurement of subsidies across age cohorts, if pension costs are to be established by relating the future benefits for all workers to the payroll received by all workers. Such an aggregation would have disguised the cost patterns observable in Figure 3.6 and Figure 3.7. To limit the extent of these cross subsidies, additional benefits of older workers could be reduced to amounts that are payable, in a larger part, by their own contributions during their remaining working years.

NOTES

1. Formally, this seems to require the replacement of a retiring employee by a new employee of 25 years old. But the representation needs to be valid on the average.

2. This amounts to "insuring" a defined benefit plan by a money purchase plan. It is being featured in some plans in practice by way of a choice exercised by terminating employees as to whether they would like to stay in the defined benefit mode or switch to the money purchase mode. Clearly, the latter is likely to be the right choice on early terminations and the former on terminations close to or at retirement.

3. See, for example, Winklevoss.

4. Since termination benefits creditable to younger employees are comparatively much more significant in MP plans than in CA plans, pension benefits in MP plans would be more dispersed under a vesting rule that includes an age requirement. For a measurement of this effect, see Balcer and Sahin, 1982.

5. For the methodology used to determine the variability and distribution of benefits, see Balcer and Sahin, 1982.

6. Recall that the benefit level in CA and FA plans is 1 percent and the contribution rate in the MP plan is 6 percent. Results under other rates will be proportional to those reported.

7. I. Sahin and Y. Balcer, *Analysis of the Impact of Proposed Reforms on the Employment Pension Plans*, Report submitted to the Budget and Intergovernmental Affairs, Ministry of Treasury and Economics, Government of Ontario, 1982.

8. *Report of the Royal Commission on the Status of Pensions in Ontario*, vol. 2, 1980, p. 79.

9. J. E. Pesando, "Private Pensions in an Inflationary Climate: Limitations and Policy Alternatives," Economic Council of Canada, Ottawa, 1979.

10. This level represents the consensus at the time of the Canadian Association of Pension Supervisory Authorities (CAPSA).

11. See note 10 above.

12. An analysis of the first policy alternative appears in Balcer and Sahin, 1984.

13. Ibid., pp. 681-686, for the methodology used.

Index

Accrued benefit, 46, 50-52, 55-59;
and earnings base, 59; under
inflation, 58, 100-102; and period
of employment, 56; and plan type,
56
Age requirement, *see* Vesting rules
Age-tenure cohorts, 50-52, 55-58, 60,
77

Balcer, Y., xiv, 79, 80, 110, 111
Base rate, 101-102
Benefit level, 6, 13, 55-56, 59, 63, 83

Canada Pension Plan (CCP), 14, 15,
67
Canadian Federal Public Service
Superannuation Administration, 68
Career average plans, 6, 13, 48, 50
53, 56-58, 61, 82; *see also*
Defined benefit plans
Cliff vesting, 4, 79, 83
Coefficient of variation, 90, 91
Committee on Corporate Pension
Funds, 11
Completed lengths of service,
distribution of, 26, 27, 28; mean
of, 26, 28; as random variables,
23-24, 32
Contribution level, 6, 15, 83
Contributory plans, 7, 83; cost rate
in, 89; cost sharing in, 16, 17,

99-100; and pension reform, 97;
plan benefits in, 86-87
Collective bargaining, and pensions,
10; and vesting rules, 12
Coverage, *see* Pension coverage
Creditable service, *see* Pensionable
service
Cross subsidies, 110

Defined benefit plans, 5, 6, 48, 50;
and age neutrality, 14, 53, 58;
benefits in, 85-87; cost of, 89-90,
98; versus defined contribution
plans, 53-55; dynamics of,
107-110; and exclusion provisions,
33; and inflation, 11, 53, 104-110;
and mobility, 64; and pension
reform, 97; returned employee
contributions in, 99; risk spreading
feature of, 54; variability of costs
and benefits under, 91-97;
and vesting rules, 65-66
Defined contribution plans, 5, 6, 48;
see also Money purchase plans
and maximum age of participation,
33; selectivity problem in, 54;
subsidy problem in, 54; and
vesting rules, 66
Dynamic analysis, 82, 97

Economic assumptions, 49, 83-84, 98

Eligibility requirements, 33, 38, 41, 50, 67; in Ontario, 13–15, 32; in the United States, 13, 32
Employer contributions, 83
Employer dynamics, and pension coverage, 27–29; and portability, 27–29; and work life pensionable service, 43–46; and work life pension benefits, 51–53

ERISA, coverage requirements under, 67; implication of, 12, 18–19, 65; participation provisions under, 12, 67; passage of, 11; vesting rules under, 4–5, 12; comparative analysis of, 32–37
Excess contributions, 83, 89, 97
Exclusion provisions, 33, 38, 41

Final average plans, 6, 8, 48, 50, 53, 56–58, 61, 82; see also Defined benefit plans
Final earnings plans, see Final average plans
Final wage plans, 50
Firm perspective, see Plan perspective
Flat benefit plans, 6, 13, 50; and inflation, 7; and unit benefit plans, 7, 48–49
Full vesting, see Cliff vesting

Graded vesting, 5, 10, 13; see also Vesting rules under ERISA, Vesting rules under Tax Reform Act of 1986
Graebner, W., 20
Greenough, W.C., 20
Guide rate, 101–102

Individual Retirement Accounts (IRAs), 3
Inflation, assumed rate of, 49, 83, 98; indexation of benefits to, 8, 11, 14; by excess interest, 16, 97, 100–103, 104–110; and pension benefits, 53, 58, 86; and pension costs, 89–90, 98
Ippolito, R.A., xiv

King, F.P., 20
Kotlikoff, L.J., 19

McDonald, M.E., 80
McGill, D.M., xiv
Mobility, 23–31; measures of, 26; models of, 24–26; and inflation indexation, 104–110; and pensionable service, 39, 41–43
Mobility, 23–31; and pension accrual, 13, 29–31; and pension benefits, 61–64, 74–78; and pension coverage, 28; and pension reform, 104–110; and plan costs, 89–90, 98; and variability of benefits and costs, 91–97; and vesting rules, 30, 42, 65
Money purchase plans, 13, 50, 56–58, 82; see also Defined contribution plans, and age-neutrality, 53, 59; cost of, 89–90; expected plan benefits under, 85, 87; variability of costs and benefits under, 91–97; versus defined benefit plans, 53–55; and inflation, 53; and mobility, 63
Mortality, assumptions of, 83; and pension benefits, 49
Multi-employer plans, 2; portability in, 3, 69; vesting rules in, 12

National Labor Relations Board, 10
Noncontributory plans, 7, 8, 83; cost of, 89–90; plan benefits in, 86–87

Ontario, Committee on Portable Pensions, 13, 15; Pension Benefits Act of 1965, 5, 14, 65; Pension Commission, 13, 14; Royal Commission on the Status of Pensions in, 14, 15, 79

Participation standards, see Eligibility requirements
Pensionable service, 4, 31–46; in the plan, 32–39; under ERISA vesting standards, 32–47; and mobility, 39;

under Tax Reform Act of 1986,
37–39; variance of, 39; and vesting
rules, 39; work life, 40–46; under
full coverage, 40–43; and mobility,
42; under partial coverage, 43–46;
and vesting rules, 41–42
Pension Benefit Guarantee
Corporation, 12
Pension benefits, 46–80; see also
Accrued benefit, Plan benefit,
Termination benefit, Virtual
benefit, Work life benefit, as
disincentives to mobility, 60, 61,
74–78; dynamics of, 104–106;
excess interest adjustment of, 97,
100–103; measurement of, 48;
and plan types, 53–61; and
vesting rules, 64–66
Pension Benefits Standards Act
of Canada, 17
Pension cost, see Plan cost
Pension coverage, 1–3, 10, 28, 67;
in Canada, 2, 12–17; and
employment dynamics, 27–28;
industrial patterns of, 2–3, 18;
in the U.S., 1–2, 7–12; and work
life pensionable service, 40–46;
and work life pension benefits,
67–74
Pension plan types, 6–7
Pension reform, 11, 16, 97;
dynamics of, 103–110;
initiatives of, 98–102
Pesando, J.E., 111
Plan benefit, 82; expected value of,
84–87; and inflation, 86; and
mobility, 85–86; and retirement
age, 85–86; and source of
contributions, 86–87; and vesting
rules, 85–86
Plan cost, 87–90, 98; computation of,
88; in contributory plans, 98–99;
distribution of, 89–97; dynamics
of, 107–110; and employee
contributions, 99; and inflation, 98,
102; and mobility, 89–90, 98; and
rate of return, 98; and retirement
age, 89–90; and plan type, 98–99;

variability of, 89–97; and vesting
rules, 89–90, 98
Plan perspective, 19, 23, 81–111
Portability, 3–4; industrial patterns of,
3; and multi-employer plans,
3, 69; Ontario legislation for,
13, 17; versus reciprocity, 68; and
work life pensionable service,
43–46; and work life pension
benefits, 67–74
Predictive period, 52
Projected benefit cost method, 88
Provincial Universal Retirement
System (PURS), 15

Qualifying service, see Pensionable
service

Railroad plans, 2, 8, 9
Rate of return, 49, 83; and base
rate, 101; and plan cost, 98
Reciprocity, 3–4, 68; see also
Portability
Registered Retirement Savings Plans
(RRSPs), 3, 16, 17
Replacement rate, 17, 48, 55–58,
62, 81, 84
Replacement ratio, see Replacement
rate
Reservation rate, 48, 50, 55–58, 62, 78
Retirement age, 27, 49–53, 81, 83,
84, 86, 88; and plan benefits, 86;
and plan costs, 89–90; and
variability of benefits and costs,
91; and vesting, 33
Returned employee contributions, 11,
16, 17, 99; see also Excess
contributions
Rule of 45, see Vesting rules
under ERISA

Sahin, I., xiii, xiv, 79, 80, 110, 111
Service requirement, see Vesting rules
Smith, D.E., 19
Social security, 8–9, 11, 17, 63, 67
Steady state analysis, 82, 97

Taft-Hartly Act, 10, 11

Tenure, in the current employment, 50, 51, 61; and mobility, 23
Termination benefit, 46, 51–52, 55, 57, 59–60; and job tenure, 60; and mobility, 63–64; and period of accumulation, 60; and plan types, 60
Termination rates, 23, 24–27; as conditional probabilities, 24; and employment dynamics, 27–28; select, 23, 24–25; ultimate, 23

Unfunded liability, 101, 110
Unit benefit plans, 6, 8, 48; see also Career average plans, Defined benefit plans, Final average plans

Vesting, 4–6, 10, 11; earlier, and portability, 67, 68; immediate, 10, 13, 15
Vesting rules, age requirement in, 2, 4, 5, 6, 10, 11, 13, 32; data on, 5–6; in early U.S. plans, 7–8, 11; under ERISA, 4–5, 12, 32–37; industrial patterns of, 5–6; under Ontario Pension Benefits Act, 5, 13–15, 16–17;

and pensionable service in the plan, 39; and pension accrual, 30; and pension benefits, 64–66; and plan costs, 89–90; in Railroad plans, 8; service requirement in, 4, 6, 7, 8, 13, 32, 40, 50, 65; under Tax Reform Act of 1986, 5, 12, 37–40; and variability of benefits and costs, 91–97; and work life pensionable service, 40–42

Virtual benefit, 46, 51–53, 55, 58, 60–61, 77; and earnings base, 61; and job tenure, 61; and mobility, 64

Wage function, 50
Wage growth rate, 49, 83, 98
Wage profile, 83
Winklevoss, H.E., 79, 110
Work life benefit, 51–53; adequacy of, 62–63; and coverage rate, 74; and mobility 61–64, 74–78; and portability, 67–74
Work life pensionable service, see Pensionable service
Work life perspective, 19, 22–80

About the Author

Izzet Sahin is Max H. Karl Professor at the School of Business Administration, University of Wisconsin-Milwaukee. In the area of pensions he has published extensively in various journals and conducted a number of studies for the Royal Commission on the Status of Pensions in Ontario (1978-79), Government of Ontario (1981-82), and the International Foundation of Employee Benefit Plans (1985). His other research interests include postemployment health care benefits and their costs in which he has recently completed a study for the International Foundation.

Professor Sahin holds an engineering degree from Technical University of Istanbul (1964), and M.S. in Management Science from Stevens Institute of Technology (1967), and a Ph.D. in Operations Research from Case Institute of Technology (1970). He has been on the editorial boards of *Operations Research* (1981-88) and *Applied Stochastic Processes and Data Analysis* (1985-). He is a member of the Institute of Management Sciences and the Operations Research Society of America.